HEMINGWAY FOR TEACHERS

92 Motivating Activities for Research and Creative Writing

by
Barbara Guthrie Teeter

© 1992
ECS Learning Systems, Inc.
P.O. Box 791437
San Antonio, Texas 78279
512-438-4262

Printed in the U.S.A.

Page Layout & Graphics: Kathryn Riches

Cover/Book Design: Educational Media Services

Other ECS activity books for Gr. 7-12 English:

Writing Warm-Ups™
Grades 7-12

Writing Warm-Ups™ Two
Grades 7-12

Quick Thinking™
Grades 7-12

Tactics to Tackle Thinking:
Creative Activities for the English Classroom 7-12

Springboards for English
Grades 6-12

Literature Guides:
American Folklore
The Canterbury Tales
The Return of the Native
To Kill a Mockingbird

To order, contact your local school supply store, or write/call:

ECS Learning Systems, Inc.
P.O. Box 791437
San Antonio, Texas 78279-1437
1-800-68-TEACH

Workshops/Institutes:
ECS provides special training at the school/district and regional level.
To schedule a workshop for your teachers, please contact ECS.

ISBN 0-944459-50-1

Give me a spirit that on life's
rough sea
Loves to have his sails filled with
a lusty wind
Even till his sailyard tremble,
his masts crack...
There is no danger to a man that knows
What life and death is–there's not
Any law
Exceeds his knowledge.

George Chapman
17th Century translator
of Homer

TABLE OF CONTENTS

ACKNOWLEDGMENTS

I thank the National Endowment for the Humanities and the Council for Basic Education for awarding me a fellowship for independent studies in the humanities two years ago. The present work grows out of my NEH research project titled *In Search of Ernest Hemingway*. I also thank Dr. Michael Reynolds, preeminent Hemingway scholar at North Carolina State University, for serving as my mentor for the NEH fellowship.

For corresponding with me about their own Hemingway studies, I express my gratitude to NEH Fellows (and fellow high school teachers) Lawrence Morwick and Peter Trenouth. Dr. Ben F. Nelms, editor of *English Journal*, was good enough to run an "Author's Query" for me concerning my work, and I heard from many Hemingway teachers from every section of the country. I thank everyone who wrote or called me, and I am particularly indebted to Vincent C. D'Amico, Alan Brown, Pamela Orth, Kay Jacob, and Maryanne Lenning.

Megan Desnoyers, curator of the Ernest Hemingway Collection at the John F. Kennedy Library, was helpful in answering my questions and was kind enough to show me two paintings from Hemingway's personal collection. Mrs. C. Maziarka, librarian at Oak Park High School (Hemingway's alma mater), was able to help me with questions concerning writings about and by Hemingway as they appeared in the publications of Oak Park and River Forest High School, 1916-1919. Barbara Ballinger, also from Oak Park, gave me some interesting insights into Hemingway juvenilia when I met her at the Hemingway In Idaho Conference last year in Sun Valley. Bernice Dickson, curator at the Hemingway Home and Museum in Key West, sent me much useful information, as did Michael Walton of the Hemingway Days Festival Committee in Key West, Florida. Greg Walz of Swank Motion Pictures and Ed Cintron of American Broadcasting Company were helpful in compiling the filmography. Allan Goodrich, archivist at the John F. Kennedy Library, helped me run down a rare copy of Hemingway's *The Spanish Earth* at the Massachusetts Institute of Technology. I also appreciate the correspondence of Robert Hamm at the National Council of Teachers of English.

For promptly answering questions and for sometimes leading me in new directions, I also thank Jean Preston, curator of manuscripts at the Ernest Hemingway Collection, Princeton University; Patricia C. Willis, The Beinecke Rare Book and Manuscript Library, Yale University; Seyed Moosavi, Harry Ransom Humanities Research Center, University of Texas; Sandra Taylor, the Lilly Library, Indiana University; and Robert Hull, Manuscripts Department, University of Virginia Library.

Finally, I thank Ann Griggs, who read my manuscript and offered many helpful suggestions.

PREFACE

Historians cite Ernest Hemingway's arrival on the literary scene in the 1920s as the beginning of a new era in American fiction. His spare and economical prose altered the stylistic tastes of his time and made him one of the brightest stars in the firmament of English letters. Hemingway preferred directness and simplicity in language, and his prose, like good poetry, was lucid, full, rich and deep. Its rhythmic beat and harmonic completeness led William Faulkner to declare that Hemingway was "a poet really, a poet through his prose." Another contemporary, Alfred Kazin, noted that Hemingway gave a whole new dimension to English prose by making it almost as exact as poetry, by making every word sound, by reaching for those places in the imagination where the word and object are one.

But it was not only Hemingway's prose that made him an American icon. Thousands bought his books for other reasons. They admired the personal Hemingway legend and the contradictions in his temperament. Here was an outdoorsman with aesthetic sensibilities—sensitive, yet brawny; brave, yet buffoonish; unconventional, yet still (as Gertrude Stein observed), the "ultimate Rotarian." Sports enthusiasts admired Hemingway's hunting and fishing exploits and his live-off-the-land ethic; counter-culturalists, including the gray-flannel suit variety, were intrigued with the so-called "Lost Generation" which Hemingway supposedly represented; and intellectuals were envious of the romantic, bohemian lifestyle he seemed to follow.

The entire world followed Hemingway's exploits—fishing and yachting in the Gulf Stream, on safari in Africa, touring the bullfight circuit in Spain, and running with the bulls in Pamplona. The public appetite for accounts of his adventures and flirtations with death, including two close calls in airplane crashes in East Africa, was insatiable.

Following the African plane crashes in 1954, Hemingway's physical and mental health deteriorated steadily. By the time he died in 1961, he was a gaunt, frail, thin, and wasted shell of man with a wistful expression and a vague smile. Broken in body and spirit, and ravaged by diabetes, depression, hypertension, hepatitis, chronic alcoholism, delusions and paranoia, he, in what one biographer called "a careful and courageous act," took his own life.

Praise came from all over the world. Hemingway's stories, it was said, were as pure and chaste as a mountain stream, as clear and crisp and perfectly shaped as icicles, as sharp as splinters of glass. No one can read Hemingway, one critic claimed, without realizing that "seldom if ever before has a writer been able to cut so deeply into life with the twenty-six curved tools of the English alphabet." *The New York Times* proclaimed that Hemingway's "shadow will long be across our continent and wherever the English language is respected."

Hemingway today is not without his detractors. Some say that he was a pitiable creature who fought demons all his life. Some claim that he was romantic about the wrong things—war, for example. Others condemn the Hemingway passion for blood sports (boxing, bull fighting, big game hunting, cock fighting) and his seemingly misogynic attitudes toward women. Still others disapprove of his posings, his self-conscious virility and exaggerated masculinity, saying that Hemingway was so unsure of his masculinity that he had to defend it with cruelty. Because of his self-doubts and self-deceptions, one critic noted that "The wildest beasts Hemingway ever confronted were those inside his head."

Still, the beauty of his work remains. Hemingway's themes of love, honor, death, courage, and endurance are universal, and his admirers everywhere seem to agree with Max Eastman, who, in summing up Hemingway's life for *The New York Times* obituary in 1961, recalled the lines by George Chapman that appear in the front leaf of this book. Eastman wrote, "That is the kind of man Hemingway tried to be, and he superbly succeeded."

Barbara Teeter
Denton, Texas
January 1, 1992

INTRODUCTION

I have long been an avid reader of Hemingway, and I have taught his five principal works to high school juniors and seniors for almost thirty years. This publication is an endeavor to share with other teachers what I have learned about Hemingway (and about teaching Hemingway) during that time, not only from personal reading and research, but from several generations of students, as well. Always, their ideas, questions and observations have piqued my interest and led me down unusual paths. Here, for example, are a few questions and ideas that have come up in class discussions. They have given me pause and made me think.

1. The Irish have a saying that sooner or later the world will break your heart. Isn't that what Hemingway is saying? Is that why we read him in high school?

2. He repackaged Ecclesiastes and sold it as *nada*.

3. I agree with William Faulkner; he really did find God at the end *(The Old Man and the Sea)*.

4. I don't think he was profound at all. What he said, you hear every day—'Life's a bitch, and then you die.'

5. He seems to think that death is the last and worst of all the practical jokes played upon us poor mortals by the gods.

6. If the strength of his prose is that it is so poetic, why is his poetry so poor?

For convenience, I shall divide my Hemingway activities into four main areas—Hemingway politics, Hemingway art, Hemingway criticism and Hemingway the man. For example, my classes explore questions such as the following:

In politics

1. Since the highest values of humanity and civilization were at stake in the Spanish Civil War, did Hemingway compromise himself as an artist by being too objective about the war *(For Whom the Bell Tolls)*?

2. How can artists who live and work with spiritual values be objective about fascism?

3. Did Hemingway forget that literature is not only the arena, but primarily the weapon, for the progress of mankind?

In art

1. Did Hemingway, as he claimed, give more depth and dimension to his prose (say, in describing landscapes) by using the pictorial techniques of Cezanne, Monet and Gauguin?

2. Do literature and art complement each other, lending each other new strength and resources?

3. Did Hemingway's personal art collection (the Miro, Gris, Klee and Braque paintings) reflect his choice of subject matter? Consider Miro's "The Farm," for example, as a reflection of Hemingway's views about Spain.

In criticism

1.   How notable is Hemingway criticism for its volume, fairness and depth?

2.   Why did Hemingway think that some scholars over-interpreted his work; that their "extravagant theories" detracted from his work?

As for Hemingway, *the man*, one student wrote, "He makes me think twice about my values. I felt terrible when I realized that I was more revolted at the thought of burying slaughtered cows than at the idea of burying dead soldiers" (*A Farewell to Arms*). Another student told his classmates that Hemingway's personal life was a shambles and a Greek tragedy. "If this is the price of genius," he said, "I'm glad to be an ordinary person."

Such observations from imaginative and creative students are evidence of the many interrelationships among art, literature, music, philosophy, history and language study. As such, they have given impetus and inspiration to this work.

DEVELOPING LITERACY THROUGH LITERATURE

As every teacher knows, challenging research projects and activities lend depth and rigor to the curriculum, encourage critical thinking, promote communication skills and invite even higher levels of reading and research. When students discover for themselves the pleasures of meaningful research and writing, they move beyond the relatively low-level skills of knowledge and comprehension to the higher levels of analysis, synthesis and evaluation. By leading students through a hierarchy of levels of thinking, we help them learn to make judgments and generalizations. By helping them become better thinkers and researchers, we help them become better thinkers as well.

Accordingly, the activities that follow are arranged around the **actual and observed** interests of youth as evidenced by the courses they take and the school clubs in which they participate. These include music, film, art and photography clubs; English, drama, and language classes and clubs; reading, travel, debate, and creative writing clubs; sports, journalism, etc.

There are many Hemingway connections and tie-ins with all of the above interest areas. For example, the young Hemingway began his writing career as a **journalist**, first as a reporter for his high school newspaper and literary magazine, then as a cub reporter for the *Kansas City Star*. That newspaper's style sheet was never far from his thoughts, and it was a major influence in the distinctive Hemingway style that later emerged. High school **language** students and members of the French, Spanish and German clubs know of Hemingway's strong connections with those countries, particularly France and Spain. **Art enthusiasts** are interested in learning about Hemingway's acknowledged debt to Cezanne, Monet and Gauguin, whose canvas techniques he applied to the printed page. **Film enthusiasts** are interested in the motion pictures that grew out of Hemingway's works. **Sports devotees** know of Hemingway's love for the outdoors. **Creative writing** students want to learn more about Hemingway's writing techniques.

It is a simple matter to derive significant research projects from the above interest areas. **Creative writing** classes, for example, show a special interest in activities No. 15, 18, 19, 28, 29, 43, 51, and 70. **Art** enthusiasts are particularly interested in activities No. 21, 28, 31, 35-37, 53, and 57. **French** and **Spanish** students and members of the **Junior Classical League** like activities No. 19, 20, and 22. **Thespians** favor activity No. 25; **Quill & Scroll** members, No. 27; **music lovers**, No. 17; **film club members**, No. 1; **camera buffs**, No. 6; **sports devotees**, No. 38, 40, and 53; **history buffs**, No. 5, 19, 30, 32, 44, 49, 58, and 66; and **travel** and **reading club enthusiasts**, No. 4, 16, 34, 38, 41, 43, 46, 59, and 60-63. Hemingway's life and works offer bounteous creative writing opportunities.

As with all research projects, it is important that students have access to an ample library with interlibrary loan services. With that advantage, teachers should find the activities that follow varied and flexible enough to be adapted to a wide range of needs for students of varying ages and abilities.

NOTES

NOTES

RESEARCH AND CREATIVE WRITING PROJECTS AND ACTIVITIES

1

Read Gene D. Phillips' *Hemingway and Film* and Frank M. Laurence's *Hemingway and the Movies*. Then view one of the Hemingway films on videocassette (see filmography) and read the corresponding book. Review and compare the print and film versions of Hemingway's work. Which is preferable, visual or verbal art? Does great literature inevitably yield great cinema, or does Hollywood tend to corrupt and trivialize literary sources? How well does Hemingway's work translate to film and what were his personal views on the subject? Facts of publication for the Phillips book are (New York: Frederick Ungar, 1980); for the Laurence book, (Jackson: University Press of Mississippi, 1981). See also Charles M. Oliver (ed) *A Moving Picture Feast: The Filmgoer's Hemingway* (New York: Praeger, 1989).

Does great literature inevitably yield great cinema, or does Hollywood tend to corrupt and trivialize literary sources?

2

Listen to *Ernest Hemingway Reading*, a rare recording of Hemingway reading his Nobel Prize acceptance speech, along with some of his poetry ("Second Poem to Mary," "In Harry's Bar," "Work In Progress," and "Saturday Night At the Whore House in Billings, Montana"). Write a composition comparing Hemingway's prose with his poetry. Do you agree with the cassette reviewer that Hemingway's "reading of this rare material is so strong, yet so personal, it's easy to imagine we're sitting across from him in his villa, relaxing in a warm Havana breeze, as he spins these marvelous pieces just for us?" Or do you agree with most critics who contend that Hemingway's prose is richer than his poetry? *Ernest Hemingway Reading* can be ordered for $9.95 from Harper & Row, 2350 Virginia Avenue, Hagerstown, Maryland 21740, toll-free number, 1-800-638-3030. The 45-minute Caedmon production (A1185 for cassette; TC1185 for long-playing record) includes background notes by Mary Hemingway and A.E. Hotchner.

3

Read the transcript of Michael Reynolds' 1971 interview with 80-year-old Agnes Von Kurowsky (Hemingway's model for Catherine in *A Farewell to Arms*) in which she recalls her relationship with the young Hemingway fifty-two years earlier. Everyone else who had been at the hospital in Milan, including Hemingway himself, was dead, and Kurowsky was seeking to "set the record straight." Compare Kurowsky's memory of the one-sided romance (she jilted him) with Hemingway's account in the novel; then write a paper titled "In Search of Catherine." The interview transcript is in Michael S. Reynolds' *Hemingway's First War: The Making of a A Farewell to Arms* (Princeton: Princeton University Press, 1976, 182-219). Also, read *Hemingway in Love and War: The Lost Diary of Agnes von Kurowsky, Her Letters and Correspondence of Ernest Hemingway* (Boston: Northeastern University Press, 1989).

4

Combine Hemingway research with summer or spring vacation plans.

(A)   For Florida travelers: Visit the Ernest Hemingway Home and Museum at 907 Whitehead Street, Key West, Florida 33040, (305) 294-1575. Write a paper on what you see there or film a 30-minute videocassette to show the class. A Registered National Historic Landmark, the Hemingway home is a tropical coralstone mansion in the Spanish colonial style surrounded by tropical plants and trees from many parts of the world, many planted by the Hemingways themselves. Furnishings, rugs, tile and chandeliers were brought by the Hemingways from Spain, Africa, and Cuba, and descendants of their fifty six-toed cats still live there. It was at this house that Hemingway wrote portions of *For Whom the Bell Tolls, Green Hills of Africa, A Farewell To Arms, The Fifth Column, The Snows of Kilimanjaro*, and *The Macomber*

© 1992 by ECS Learning Systems, Inc., San Antonio, Texas

Affair. See pictures of the home in advance in *Architectural Digest*, January, 1981. Also while in Key West, see Sloppy Joe's bar, which figures in many Hemingway stories. The "Papa Doble" is still served there. Write ahead to HEMINGWAY DAYS FESTIVAL, Box 4045, Key West 33041 for dates for this year's festival celebrating the man, his works, and the writing profession. The festival centers around Sloppy Joe's and includes a street fair, food-fest, look-alike contest, etc. (Note: Visit other literary shrines while in Key West. Both Tennessee Williams and Truman Capote had Key West connections).

(B)   For Boston and New England travelers: Visit the John F. Kennedy Library, which houses a large collection of Hemingway correspondence, manuscripts, exhibits, artifacts, and memorabilia. Write a composition on what you see there. The address is JFK Library, Columbia Point, Boston 02125, (617) 929-4500. Other Hemingway collections are at Firestone Library/Princeton and Beinecke Library/Yale. Firestone has about 1,000 Hemingway letters.

5

Write Dr. Robert W. Lewis, president of the Hemingway Society, University of North Dakota, Grand Forks, ND 58202 for information as to what role *junior* scholars might play in future activities. The Society (about 350 members) publishes two issues a year of *The Hemingway Review* and *The Hemingway Newsletter* (most back issues of both *The Hemingway Review* and *Hemingway Notes,* predecessor to *The Hemingway Review*, are available). The society meets annually between Christmas and New Year's, and sponsors an international conference every two years at locations which figure prominently in the Hemingway saga (Paris, Schruns, Pamplona, etc.). Membership is $18 per year and includes subscriptions to the above publications. Obtain literature concerning the Society as well as back issues of the *Review* and the *Newsletter*; then write a composition on the publications, history, and accomplishments of the Society.

6

Assemble a photo-essay titled "Life with Papa." Prints of thousands of the best photographs of Hemingway are available at reasonable rates from the JFK Library, telephone (617) 929-4500. Categories include Hemingway's father's collection 1888-1903; the early years 1899-1921; the Paris years 1922-30; wars 1917-45; Key West years 1928-1939; Wyoming 1928-1937; Idaho 1939-61; and Africa, Europe, Cuba, Spain, and miscellaneous. For ideas as to what constitutes a good photo-essay, see one of the best done to date on Hemingway, *Life* Magazine, July 14, 1961, cover and pages 59-71. The essay contains what Hemingway called "the best picture I ever had taken," (walking along an Idaho roadside at age sixty, kicking a can high in the air). Others believe the *Life* cover picture is best. For pictures of the Hemingway home at Ketchum, Idaho, see *Architectural Digest*, April, 1988. The best photo-biography of Hemingway is Peter Buckley's *Ernest* (New York: Dial Press, 1978). Mary Hemingway, Buckley's friend for twenty-five years, gave him permission to choose from her collection of more than 10,000 photographs. With a close-up lens or a more expensive macro lens, you can photograph these pictures and display them in class.

7

Listen to Charleton Heston read selections from *The Old Man and the Sea,* and write a review giving your impressions of Hemingway's prose. Copies of the two cassettes (A2084) can be ordered from Harper and Row, 2350 Virginia Avenue, Hagerstown, Maryland 21740, toll-free number, 1-800-638-3030; or from Caedmon Records, 1995 Broadway, New York 10023, telephone (212) 580-3400. The cost is $14.95. For an excellent discussion of *The Old Man and the Sea*, listen to "Discussion Leader Cassette: Old Man & Sea," available for $5.95 from Spectrum Educational Media, P.O. Box 611, Mattoon, Illinois 61938. Also, read and comment on Gurney Williams' "Programming Papa," (*Science Digest*, 77 June 1975, 56-57). Using computer analysis, the author claims that excerpts from *The Old Man and the Sea* are closer in sentence length to Hemingway's writing done in the mid 1930s than that done in the 1940s and 1950s, and hypothesizes that much of *Old Man* was written during the mid 1930s (before the erosion of Hemingway's writing talents).

8

Write a composition giving your impressions of Max Eastman's parody, "Bull in the Afternoon," in *New Republic*, June 7, 1933, 94-97. This is the famous essay ("Come out from behind that false hair on your chest, Ernie, we all know who you are.") that caused the fistfight between Hemingway and Eastman in Maxwell Perkins' office at Scribner's. See also "Hemingway Slaps Eastman in Face," and "Eastman Claims Title in Literary Slug Fest," *The New York Times*, August 14, 15, and 16, 1937. See pages 15, 31, and 21.

"Come out from behind that false hair on your chest, Ernie, we all know who you are."

9

Read *A Farewell to Arms;* then invent your own title, using, as Hemingway did, *The Oxford Book of English Verse* for ideas. Defend your choice in a brief essay. Then search 17th Century poet Andrew Marvell's poem "To His Coy Mistress" for another substitute title (since Hemingway used two lines from the poem in Chapter 23 of *A Farewell to Arms*). Possible titles from this source include *World Enough and Time, Long Love's Day, Time's Winged Chariot,* and *A Fine and Private Place.* Would any of these phrases have made more sense as a title for *A Farewell to Arms*? Why does *A Fine and Private Place* sound so much like Hemingway? Explain in a brief essay. (Note: Hemingway considered *World Enough and Time* as a title. He also considered *The Italian Journey, Love in War, Late Wisdom, The Italian Experience, If You Must Love,* and *In Praise of His Mistress.*)

10

In *A Farewell to Arms*, Frederic quotes two lines from Andrew Marvell's "To His Coy Mistress" as he and Catherine wait for what could be their final parting. Catherine replies, "I know that poem. It's by Marvell...It's about a girl who wouldn't live with a man." Explicate the poem and write a paper speculating as to the possible tie-in in Hemingway's mind between the poem and the novel. The two-line quotation is

But at my back I always hear
Time's winged chariot hurrying near

11

Dedicated to Queen Elizabeth I, George Peele's 16th Century poem, *A Farewell to Arms* would become the source of Hemingway's title. Explicate the poem. (Note: A swain is a male admirer or suitor; a beadsman is one who prays for another.)

12

Archibald MacLeish, a famous poet and erstwhile Hemingway friend, wrote the following poem in which there was both a question about Hemingway and an answer. Explicate the poem after reading MacLeish's "His Mirror Was Danger," *Life* Magazine, July 14, 1961, pages 71-72. What did MacLeish mean by "Fame became of him"?

What did MacLeish mean by "Fame became of him"?

> ...the lad in the Rue de Notre Dame des Champs
> In the carpenter's loft on the left-handed side going
> down—
> The lad with the supple look like a sleepy
> panther—
> And what became of him? Fame became of him.
> Veteran out of the wars before he was twenty:
> Famous at twenty-five: thirty a master—
> Whittled a style for his time from a walnut stick
> In a carpenter's loft in a street of that April city.

The poem is in MacLeish's "Year of the Dog," *ACT FIVE and Other Poems* (n.p.: Random House, 1948).

13

One of the most enduring adolescents in American fiction is Holden Caulfield, the protagonist in J.D. Salinger's *Catcher In The Rye*. Clear-visioned and morally acute, Holden declared both *A Farewell to Arms* and Frederic Henry, its main character, to be "phony." Holden could not understand how anyone could profess a moral revulsion against war and at the same time like the book and its main character. Write a composition supporting or rebutting Holden's reasoning. First, read *Catcher*.

14

Keep in mind that artists create and rearrange their experiences and filter these experiences through their imaginations.

Hemingway told A.E. Hotchner in 1954, "What happened between the Red Cross nurse (Agnes Von Kurowsky, the model for Catherine in *A Farewell to Arms*) and me is pretty much as I wrote it in 'A Very Short Story.'" Exactly two pages long and written in 1927, this story compresses the essence of what would later become *A Farewell to Arms*. "Now I Lay Me," also written in 1927, further sets the stage for the larger work that appeared two years later. Write a composition showing how *A Farewell to Arms*, "A Very Short Story," and "Now I Lay Me" conform (or do not conform) to actual events as related by the eighty-year-old Agnes Von Kurowsky in her 1971 interview with Michael S. Reynolds. Keep in mind that artists create and rearrange their experiences and filter these experiences through their imaginations. See Michael Reynolds' *Hemingway's First War: The Making of A Farewell to Arms* (Princeton: Princeton University Press, 1976, 182-219).

15

Write a creative screenscript in which the wounded Lt. Henry in *A Farewell to Arms* awakens to find himself, not in a Milan hospital, but recovering from "meatball surgery" in "post-op" at MASH 4077. Substitute Father Mulcahy for the priest and nurse Margaret Houlihan for Catherine. Rinaldi can be either Trapper John, B.J. Hunnicut, Charles Emerson Winchester III, or Major Frank Burns. The challenge is to remain faithful to the MASH personalities—a " humorless" Houlihan/Catherine, a "superior" Charles, a "villainous" Frank, a "fun-loving" Trapper John. (Note: B.J. Hunnicut—gentle wit, faithful, unjudgmental, ideal husband, etc.—provides the most striking contrast to the bawdy, womanizing Rinaldi.)

16

The following preface to Erich Remarque's *All Quiet on the Western Front* sums up not only his book, written from the perspective of a German soldier in World War I, but also the "other side" books of Henri Barbusse (*Under Fire: The Story of a Squad*, written from the perspective of a French soldier in World War I) and Ernest Hemingway (*A Farewell to Arms*, written from the perspective of American and Italian soldiers in World War I):

> This book is neither an accusation nor a confession, and least of all an adventure, for death is not an adventure to those who stand face to face with it. It will try simply to tell of a generation of men who, even though they may have escaped its shells, were destroyed by the war.

Read the three books and view the *All Quiet* and *Farewell* videocassettes; then write a composition on whether Hemingway and the "Lost Generation" he supposedly represented were ultimately destroyed by World War I even though they escaped its shells. Write another composition on the common thoughts of 18-year-old soldiers in combat, no matter which side they happen to be on. Remarque's book was published by Little Brown & Co in Boston, 1929, the year Scribner's brought out *A Farewell to Arms*. Barbusse's book was published by Dutton in 1917.

... for death is not an adventure to those who stand face to face with it.

17

The moving picture industry did not develop in time to play a role in generating public support for World War I (as it did for World War II). The music industry did play a role, however, by contributing many light-hearted songs promising travel and adventure to youth like the 18-year-old Ernest Hemingway. Such songs include "Good-Bye Broadway: Hello France!," "Mademoiselle From Armentiers," "It's A Long Way to Tipperary," "Over There," and "Grand Old Flag." Read Kent Bowman's "Echoes of Shot and Shell: Songs of the Great War" (*Studies In Popular Culture* X:1, 1987, 27-41) and call the Library of Congress Archive of National Music in Washington, D.C. (202) 707-5000 for further background help. Then assemble a collection of sound recordings that re-create the spirit of the times for World War I. Play a medley of these tunes in class as an introduction to reading *A Farewell to Arms*.

18

It is possible to improve your writing skills by trying some of the writing techniques Hemingway himself used. For example, Hemingway sometimes spaced several times between words

so   that   the   page   looked   like   this.   He   did
this   to   emphasize   the   importance   of
each   word.

Other techniques included writing "slowly and deliberately"; "telling the whole truth about things, holding nothing back"; writing **only** "in disciplined isolation," i.e., alone with no distractions; writing **only** in the mornings (beginning very early); beginning by reading everything already written from the start; and writing and re-writing until it was finally right. (The ending to *A Farewell to Arms* was written 39 times in manuscript and 30 more times in proof.) Hemingway also advised writers to read widely and study the best literary models; to master their subject through experience and reading; and to work continually on a project once it had been started. Hemingway cautioned writers not to discuss material while writing about it; to stop writing when things were going well so that there would be sufficient momentum to continue the next day; and not to think about writing when finished for the day, but to allow the subconscious mind to ponder what had been written. Hemingway was "ruthless with himself," wrote a friend.

Try some of the above ideas as you write a paper titled "The Craft of Writing—by Ernest Hemingstein." ("Stein," Hemingway's high school nickname, originated with his piece in the school newspaper—*The Trapeze*—titled "Hemingway and a Full Stein." This eve-of-prohibition satirical piece by a sixteen-year-old bordered on impropriety at the time.)

The ending to A Farewell to Arms *was written 39 times in manuscript and 30 more times in proof.*

19

In thirty-four moving words, Hemingway summed up the Paris he knew between 1922-1930:

> If you are lucky enough to have lived in Paris as a young man, then wherever you go for the rest of your life it stays with you, for Paris is a moveable feast.

...Paris is a moveable feast.

Write a paper imaginatively re-creating Paris scenes of the 1920s as Hemingway described them in his writings. One of the best evocations of those years is in Robert E. Gajdusek's *Hemingway's Paris* (NY: Charles Scribner's Son, 1978). This 180-page photo-essay recaptures Hemingway's favorite spots, i.e., the bridges, bookstalls, statues, cafes, bars, bistros, studios and flats mentioned in his works, including the Dingo and Le Select American bars, the Cafe de Flore, Gertrude Stein's studio apartment, Sylvia Beach's Shakespeare and Company, Le Negre de Toulouse where the Hemingways frequently dined, and the night life resorts of Montmartre and Montparnasse. Also pictured are scenes from the Luxembourg Gardens (with pigeons such as those caught for food by Hemingway during one lean Paris winter); the Rue Notre-Dame-des Champs, where the Hemingways lived; and street scenes along walks made famous by the Hemingways and by Jake Barnes and Bill Gorton in *The Sun Also Rises*—the artichoke stands, bookstalls, fishmarkets, bakers' carts filled with long loaves of bread, and Parisians fishing along the Seine. For more of the ambiance of Paris and the spirit of the times, see John Leland's *A Guide to Hemingway's Paris* (Chapel Hill, NC: Algonquin Books of Chapel Hill, 1989) and read Morley Callaghan's *That Summer in Paris* (New York: Coward-McCann, 1963) and John Dos Passos' *The Best Times* (New York: New American Library, 1966). If you belong to the French Club, write your essay in French. Title it, "We'll Always Have Paris" (the famous line from *Casablanca*) or "That April City" (from Archibald MacLeish's poem about Hemingway in MacLeish's *ACT FIVE and Other Poems,* Random House, 1948).

20

Hemingway called Spain "the country that I loved more than any other except my own..."

Hemingway called Spain "the country that I loved more than any other except my own," and captured the spirit and flavor of the country in his prose by creating many beautiful images—Basque shepherds tending their flocks; spirited crowds caught up in fiesta fervor; the sounds of church bells and the clopping of mules and burros on cobblestones; delicately perfumed summer nights, etc. Write a paper imaginatively re-creating Hemingway's Spain as he described it in his writings. One of the best evocations of Spain is Barnaby Conrad's *Hemingway's Spain* with photographs by Loomis Dean (San Francisco Books, 1989). Another is the film *SPAIN: Everything Under the Sun*. The 50-minute videocassette featuring Madrid, La Prado, El Escorial, Toledo, Alhambra, Costa del Sol and Barcelona can be ordered from Book-of-the-Month Video, Camp Hill, Pennsylvania 17012-001. The catalog VHS number is 44-6224 and the price is $24.95. Lester Cooper's television film "Hemingway in Spain" cannot be rented or purchased, but a copy can possibly be borrowed for school use from the ABC Television Network in New York. See also *Life* Magazine, September 5, 1960, 77; and William White's *Ernest Hemingway—Dateline: Toronto* (New York: Charles Scribner's Sons, 1985, 106). If you belong to the Spanish Club, write your essay in Spanish. Title it *Iberia* (from James Mitchner's famous book).

21

Hemingway's personal favorite image of Spain was Joan Miro's "The Farm" ("La Granja"), which now hangs in the National Gallery of Art in Washington, D.C. He owned the painting, lived with it and loved it for 30 years; he said that it "has in it all that you feel about Spain when you are there and all that you feel when you are away and cannot go there." Write the National Gallery for a photograph or print (or obtain one from your art teacher), and write a paper describing your own reactions to Miro's work (surreal, imaginative, freely drawn, etc.). If possible, visit the National Gallery (open to the public free of charge every day except Christmas and New Year's Day) and write a paper describing your reactions to (a) "La Granja" and (b) the classically designed National Gallery.

22

Even though Hemingway learned languages easily (he was fluent in Spanish, French and Italian), his lowest grades in high school were in Latin where he earned a three-semester average of 73. Invent a humorous reason for this and write a parody in the Hemingway style explaining the reason. The challenge is to make the composition sound like Hemingway and read like Hemingway. If you belong to the Classical League, write in Latin and irreverently title your work *"Purgamentum Init. Exit Purgamentum."*

23

Submit an entry in the short story competition in this summer's Hemingway Days Festival at Key West. Send your unpublished, typed fiction manuscript of 2,500 words or fewer and a $10 entry fee for each story by June 1 to Hemingway Days Festival, P.O. Box 4045, Key West, Florida 33041. Manuscripts are not returned. (Note: "Six Stories," a compilation of the winning stories from the first six years of the contest, is available from the same address.)

24

Write the Hemingway Foundation of Oak Park, Illinois, c/o Lily Bolero, P.O. Box 423, Hinsdale, Illinois 60522-0423 for information concerning next summer's Fiesta de Hemingway competition in Oak Park. Ten prizes, including two first-class airline tickers to Pamplona, Spain, were awarded at the Fiesta's first year's competition. The task that year was to view a historic photograph of Hemingway talking to Fidel Castro, and to then write a caption revealing what Hemingway might have been saying to Castro. Judges (they included novelist Kurt Vonnegut) looked for captions showing literary, historical, and political acumen, as well as humor. The photograph and winning caption were then laser printed on T-shirts and sold commercially, with proceeds going to the Hemingway Foundation for eventual purchase of the Hemingway boyhood home in Oak Park.

25

Stage an amateur production of "The Lost Generation," a drama written by Hilary Hemingway and Jeffry Freundlich. The story is based in Paris during the 1920s and explores the lives of Ernest Hemingway, Alice B. Toklas, Gertrude Stein, and Hadley Richardson, Hemingway's first wife. The 1920s were formative years for these talented individuals, and the time they spent together was researched by the authors. For information on obtaining the script, write "HDF," 424 Fleming Street, Key West, Florida 33041.

26

Compose a Hemingway trivia quiz including little-known facts about Hemingway's novels and personal life. First, listen to "Robert Stack Reads A.E. Hotchner's *Papa Hemingway*" (available at $11.95 from Listen for Pleasure, Ltd., 111 Martin Ross Avenue, Downsview, Ontario, Canada M3J2M1) and "Ernest Hemingway: Author Analysis Cassettes" (available at $6.95 from Spectrum Educational Media, Mattoon, Illinois 61938). Submit questions, answers and documentation to Radio Station FM 107 WIIS, Key West, Florida 33041. There are no prizes, but contributions are publicly acknowledged at the Hemingway Days Festival and may receive notice in the *Hemingway Newsletter*.

27

Enter the competition for the Hemingway Journalism Award held annually in conjunction with the Hemingway Days Festival. Applicants should submit **only** work **published** prior to June 1st of each year. The awards program is intended to encourage excellence in journalism. Judging emphasis is placed on humanistic and experiential writing and on personal and experiential reporting. Categories include news, features, sports and the arts. For more information, write "HDF," 424 Fleming Street, Key West, Florida 33041, or call (305) 294-4440.

28

Hemingway maintained that he learned to give more depth and dimension to his prose by using Cezanne's pictorial techniques, and that he learned everything he knew about describing landscapes from studying Cezanne, Monet and Gauguin. Do the arts tend to complement and substitute for one another by lending each other new strength and resources? Read Robert Lair, "Hemingway and Cezanne: An Indebtedness," *Modern Fiction Studies*, 6 (1960), 165-168; Meyly Hagemann, "Hemingway's Secret: Visual to Verbal Art," *Journal of Modern Literature*, 7 (1979), 87-112; Raymond S. Nelson, *Hemingway: Expressionist Artist* (Iowa State University Press, 1979) and Jeffrey Meyers, *Painting and the Novel* (Manchester: Manchester University Press, 1975). Write a paper reacting to Meyers' statement that

> comparisons with works of art in the modern
> novel are similar to the literary use of metaphor,
> symbol, archetype or myth, for they evoke a
> new depth of meaning through suggestive allusion.

29

Hemingway drew many unforgettable portraits of his contemporaries in Paris following World War I. Some of these expatriates are now familiar names in American letters (Ezra Pound, Ford Madox Ford, F. Scott Fitzgerald, etc.). Read Hemingway's *A Moveable Feast;* then read the other works listed below and write a paper comparing the Hemingway memoir with the remembrances of others who were there. Some famous memoirists and their works include John Glassco, *Memoirs of Montparnasse* (Toronto: Oxford University Press, 1970); James R. Mellow, *Charmed Circle: Gertrude Stein and Company* (New York: Praeger, 1974); Arthur Mizener, *The Saddest Story: A Biography of Ford Madox Ford* (New York: World, 1971); Peter Ackroyd, *Ezra Pound and His World* (New York: Scribner's, 1980); and John Dos Passos, *The Best Times* (New York: New American Library, 1966). See also George Wickes, *Americans in Paris (*New York: Doubleday, 1969); James Charters, *This Must Be the Place*: *Memoirs of Montparnasse* (London: H. Joseph, 1934); and Harold Loeb, *The Way It Was* (New York: Criterion, 1959). (Loeb was Robert Cohn in *The Sun Also Rises*.)

Do the arts tend to complement and substitute for one another by lending each other new strength and resources?

30

Some of the bloodiest battles mankind has ever known were fought in World War I, the setting for *A Farewell to Arms*. For vivid recreations of that war, see a photo-essay on the shell-pocked, gas-choked inferno of the Western Front in a two-part series in *Life* Magazine, March 13 and 20, 1964. Read also Barbara Tuchman's *The Guns of August* (New York: Dell, 1963); Laurence Stallings, *The First World War: A Photographic History* (New York: Simon & Schuster, 1933); and Paul Fussell, *The Great War and Modern Memory* (New York; Oxford University Press, 1975). Then, reproduce selected photographs from the essays and create a slide show with an accompanying audiotape on World War I. Use the slide show in class as an introduction to a *A Farewell to Arms*.

Some of the bloodiest battles mankind has ever known were fought in World War I, the setting for A Farewell to Arms.

31

Read or view *Andre Masson: The Pictorial Catalog* (Oxford: Clarendon Press, 1981); Raymond Cogniat, *Georges Braque* (New York: H.N. Abrams, 1980); *The Graphic Legacy of Paul Klee* (Annandale-on-Hudson, New York: Bard College, 1983); and *Illustrations of the Juan Gris Exhibition at the Juan Gris University Art Museum,* University of California, Berkeley (New York; Abbeville Press, 1983). Then assemble a selection of prints and photographs of the most important works in Hemingway's art collection. Include the Georges Braque paintings as well as Joan Miro's "The Farm"; Juan Gris' "The Guitarist" and "The Torero"; Paul Klee's "Monument in Arbeit"; and Andre Masson's "Dice Game," "Land with Trees," "Killed Animals," and "The Little Pond." Prepare an exhibition of these works for class and invite an art critic or historian to talk to your class about the works and their significance.

32

The Italian army suffered a gruesome defeat by the Germans at Caporetto in the fall of 1917, but, after losing thousands of men, finally stopped the enemy along the Piave River. Hemingway wrote vividly of the carnage at Caporetto in *A Farewell to Arms*. Read about the **real** battle in Cyril Fall's *The Battle of Caporetto* (Philadelphia: Lippincott, 1966). Then write a paper pointing out the similarities and differences between the **fictional** account provided by Hemingway and the **actual** events, including the weather. (Rain is an important symbol in *A Farewell to Arms.)*

33

According to Jeffrey Meyers ("Wanted by the FBI!," *New York Review of Books,* March 31, 1983, 17-20), the FBI never forgave Hemingway for his support of the Loyalist cause in the Spanish Civil War. Believing him to have communist leanings (although no evidence was or could be offered to prove it), "the Bureau made unsuccessful attempts to control, mock, and vilify him." Hemingway's FBI file, maintained from 1942 until after his death, ultimately contained 124 pages, fifteen of which are still withheld "in the interests of national security." Are such surveillance activities tantamount to government censorship of art, or do they in the long run provide a climate of freedom in which art can flourish? Write a position paper taking either side.

Hemingway wrote vividly of the carnage at Caporetto in A Farewell to Arms.

34

Write a paper on the contents of the Hemingway Collection at the John F. Kennedy Library in Boston. What is available there in terms of Hemingway's personal art collection, game trophies, manuscripts, photographs, correspondence, newspaper clippings, scrapbooks, high school doodles and other souvenirs and remembrances from Hemingway's life? Visit the library if possible, but also read Jo August's "Hemingway at Columbia Point: The Kennedy Library Holdings," *Wilson Library Bulletin*, December, 1980, v. 55, #4, 267-271. Also, write or call Megan Floyd Desnoyers, JFK Library, Columbia Point, Boston, MA 02125 (617) 929-4524 for information on recent Hemingway collection acquisitions. Note: The *Wilson Library Bulletin* is published monthly except in July and August by The H.W. Wilson Company, 950 University Avenue, Bronx, New York 10452.

35

The "girl" Hemingway loved longer than any other in his life, according to one associate, was Andrea del Sarto's "Portrait of a Woman," which hangs at *La Prado* in Madrid. Locate a print or a photograph of this sixteenth century painting, and write a paper explaining what Hemingway's fascination with her might have been. First read Carlos Baker's ruminations about "Hemingway women" in his *Ernest Hemingway: Critiques of Four Major Novels* (New York: Charles Scribner's Sons, 1962, 55-60). See also Bernice Kert, *The Hemingway Women* (New York: W.W. Norton, 1983); Roger Whitlow's *Cassandra's Daughters: The Women in Hemingway* (Westport, Conn.: Greenwood Press, 1984); and A. E. Hotchner's *Papa Hemingway: The Ecstasy and Sorrow* (New York: William Morrow, 1983, 187-88).

The "girl" Hemingway loved longer than any other in his life, according to one associate, was Andrea del Sarto's "Portrait of a Woman," which hangs at La Prado *in Madrid.*

36

Madrid's *La Prado* (National Museum of Painting and Sculpture) still contains many of the paintings Hemingway most admired including Andrea del Sarto's "Portrait of a Woman." View the film, *A Tour of the Prado*; then write a paper on the major holdings of this treasure house of art. Hemingway especially liked the works of El Greco, Goya, and Diego Velazquez. Which do you like best and why? The sixty-minute videocassette, *A Tour of the Prado*, can be ordered from the Book-of-the-Month Video, Camp Hill, Pennsylvania 17012-0001. Ask for catalog #VHS 53-6424. The cost is $27.95.

37

The Louvre in Paris is the largest art museum in the world, and along with Madrid's *La Prado*, was one of Hemingway's favorite haunts. View the film *A Tour of the Louvre*; then write a description of the museum's major holdings including Hemingway favorites "Winged Victory," "Mona Lisa," and "Venus de Milo." The 105-minute videocassette, *A Tour of the Louvre*, can be ordered for $27.95 from Book-of-the-Month Video, Camp Hill, Pennsylvania 17012-0001. Ask for catalog #VHS 33-6422.

38

Hemingway went to Spain in 1959 to watch the country's two greatest matadors engage in a series of deadly combats known as **mano a manos**. True **mano a manos** are rare since seldom are two great matadors fighting concurrently. Read A.E. Hotchner's account of this "dangerous summer" when the aging Luis Miguel Dominguin went **mano a manos** against Antonio Ordonez, whom many thought even more talented than Manolete, the greatest bullfighter of all time. It is interesting that Ordonez's father had been the prototype for the matador in Hemingway's *The Sun Also Rises,* published thirty-two years earlier. Write a paper about the outcome of this "dual to the death," but first see the seventy-six-page pictorial essay on the duel in *Life,* September 5, 12, and 19, 1960. Then read chapter 12 of A.E. Hotchner's *Papa Hemingway: The Ecstasy and Sorrow* (New York: William Morrow, 1983).

39

As a cub reporter for the *Toronto Star,* the young Hemingway wrote 172 stories which are now collected in William White's *Ernest Hemingway—DATELINE: TORONTO The Complete 'Toronto Star' Dispatches, 1920-1924* (New York: Charles Scribner's Sons, 1985). Read these dispatches and write a paper commenting on the journalistic talents of Hemingway, then in his early twenties. Is Hemingway's passion for the "inside story," or what he called the "true gen" (true intelligence) apparent in his early writing career? Comment on the freshness of these stories today (more than sixty-five years after publication). Also comment specifically on: "Store Thieves' Tricks," "Rum Running," "Wild Night Music of Paris," "The Big Dance on the Hill," and "The Blind Man's Christmas Eve."

40

Hemingway's affinity for the outdoors is unmistakable in his *Toronto Star* dispatches on the subjects of deer hunting, duck shooting, trout fishing, prizefighting, horse racing, bobsledding, etc. Read several of his sports stories in William White's *Ernest Hemingway—DATELINE: TORONTO The Complete 'Toronto Star' Dispatches, 1920-1924* (New York: Charles Scribner's Sons, 1985). Then write a paper commenting on your favorite pieces. Include comments on

*Hemingway went to Spain in 1959 to watch the country's two greatest matadors engage in a series of deadly combats known as **mano a manos**.*

"Trout-Fishing Hints," "Camping Out: When You Camp Out, Do It Right," "The Sport of Kings," "Tuna Fishing in Spain," "Try Bobsledding if You Want Thrills," "Fishing at the Rhone Canal," and "Game Shooting in Europe." Hemingway also contributed twenty-five articles on hunting, fishing, and traveling to *Esquire* magazine between 1933-1936. Read these pieces and comment on several of them in your paper.

41

Finca Vigia (Lookout Farm), Hemingway's Cuban home for 22 years, and now one of that country's most popular museums, remains essentially as the Hemingways left it. (For a complete inventory of the museum's thousands of pieces, see Norberto Fuentes' *Hemingway in Cuba*, Secausus, N.J.: Lyle Stuart, 1984, 436-445). Although the museum is within field trip distance for thousands of American junior scholars, it cannot be visited by American citizens by provision of the U.S. Department of the Treasury's *Cuban/Assets Control Regulations,* Chapter V, Title 31, part 515.560, section h2 and h3. American high school students are specifically denied permission to visit the Hemingway home-museum-library by the above regulations which state that

> Study visits to Cuba in connection with pre-college or undergraduate college course work are not within the scope of professional research and similar activities authorized by the general license.

> Categories for travel which…will normally be denied include recreational travel; tourist travel; travel in pursuit of a hobby; general study tours; general orientation visits; student class field trips; youth camps; research for personal satisfaction only, etc.

Investigate the pros and cons of this government policy, which has been in effect since 1962, in a debate—Resolved: That as free people, United States citizens have (do not **necessarily** have) the right to travel where they please. For background reading, write the Treasury Department, Washington, D.C., for a copy of the above regulations; then write the U.S. Department of State, Bureau of Consular

American high school students are specifically denied permission to visit the Hemingway home-museum-library.

Affairs, Washington, D.C., for "Tips for Travelers to Cuba" (publication #9232) and "Foreign Visa Requirements" (publication M-264). Also write your elected representatives in Congress for their positions on the policy and for information as to why we have such policies and how (if you disagree with them) they can be changed.

42

A group of high school students once asked Hemingway how he had learned the languages he knew. He replied that his high school Latin had made language-learning easier but that **actually living** abroad and reading the newspapers (English in the morning, the new language being learned in the afternoon) was the best way to learn a language. Motivated high school students can arrange to live abroad on an exchange basis for a few weeks, a summer, or entire academic year. Gather information from the sources below on how this can be accomplished; then present the information to your class in an oral report. First, write or call The Council on Standards for International Educational Travel, 1906 Association Drive, Reston, Virginia 22091 (703) 860-5317, for a booklet entitled *Advisory List of International Educational Travel and Exchange Programs*. This is a comprehensive listing of the most desirable exchange programs available (all are certified). Also write or call The Council on International Educational Exchange, 205 East 42nd Street, New York 10017 (212) 661-1414, and ask for the current edition of *The Teenager's Guide to Study, Travel, and Adventure Abroad*. This guide describes more than 150 programs and includes interviews with youth who have participated in the programs as well as information for parents, teachers, and counselors. The guide costs $8.95. Also call or write The International Youth Exchange Staff, U.S. Information Agency, 301 4th Street SW, Room 357, Washington, D.C. 20547 (202) 485-7299. If you are interested in Spain, the country Hemingway "loved more than any other" except his own, write or call the Iberoamerican Cultural Exchange Program, 13920 93rd Avenue, Dept. CS, Kirkland, Washington 98034 (206) 821-1463. Under this program, high school students spend six weeks during the summer in Spain—three weeks in Zaragoza and three weeks in Madrid. The program includes a home stay with a Spanish family for the full six weeks, intensive Spanish language classes three hours per day, and afternoon and weekend excursions.

A group of high school students once asked Hemingway how he had learned the languages he knew.

43

The best way to condense a classic, Hemingway continued, would be to reduce it to a newspaper headline...

As a cub reporter for the *Toronto Star*, twenty-two-year-old Ernest Hemingway wrote a mirthful piece titled "Condensing the Classics." It was a put-down of publishers who condense the great literature of the world into "palatable morsels for the tired businessman's consumption." Hemingway chided the condenser-publishers for cutting *Les Miserables* to ten pages; *Don Quixote* to a column and a half; and Shakespeare's plays to 800 words each. Even the *Iliad* and the *Odyssey* were reduced, Hemingway pointed out, and although it was a "splendid thing" to bring the classics within the grasp of tired businessmen, there was an even quicker way to present culture to those "who must run while reading." The best way to condense a classic, Hemingway continued, would be to reduce it to a newspaper headline followed by a short news story giving the gist of the matter. As an example, Hemingway reduced *Don Quixote* to the headline, "CRAZED KNIGHT IN WEIRD TILT," followed by a two-sentence summary of the story. *Othello* was reduced to "SLAYS HIS WHITE BRIDE—SOCIETY GIRL WED TO AFRICAN WAR HERO FOUND STRANGLED IN BED," followed by a four-sentence summary. Works by William Blake and Samuel Coleridge were similarly reduced. Taking your cue from Hemingway's tongue-in-cheek journalism, write similar headlines and news stories for several literary classics of your choosing. See Hemingway's *Toronto Star* story in William White's *Ernest Hemingway—DATELINE: TORONTO* (New York: Charles Scribner's Sons, 1985, 78-80).

44

On New Year's Day, 1959, Colonel Fulgencio Batista fled Havana, and Fidel Castro took over the capital. When the *New York Times* telephoned Hemingway for comment, he said that he was "delighted" with the revolution and that he believed in its "historical necessity" and "long-range aims." In a separate interview, he said that Cuba had finally had "a decent moment in history." Hemingway never recanted his words, even though the Castro government expropriated most of his Cuban property including his home *Finca Vigia* (Lookout Farm) and *Pilar,* his fishing yacht. Write a paper agreeing or disagreeing with Hemingway's position on Cuba (remember that he died before the revolution's third anniversary). First read Carlos Franqui, *Diary of the Cuban Revolution* (New York: Viking Press, 1980); Jay Mallin (ed.), *"Che" Guevara on Revolution* (New York: Dell, 1970); and Tad Szulc, *Fidel: A Critical Portrait* (New York: Avon Books, 1986). See also Mary Welsh Hemingway's *How It Was* (New York: Alfred A. Knopf, 1976, 458) and Norberto Fuentes' *Hemingway in Cuba* (Secaucus, N.J.: Lyle Stuart, 1984, 271).

45

On April 10, 1964, *Life* magazine published a 32-page pictorial essay evoking the Paris of Hemingway's "lost generation" (a romantic concept that Hemingway poked fun at but nevertheless capitalized on). The essay includes excerpts from *A Moveable Feast* and scenes from Sylvia Beach's famous Shakespeare and Company book shop, the meeting place of Hemingway's artist and writer friends. Read the essay and John Raeburn's *Fame Became of Him: Hemingway as Public Writer* (Bloomington: Indiana University Press, 1984). Also read Mary Hemingway's *How It Was* (New York: Alfred A. Knopf, 1976, 263, 284, 315, 386, 401-413); and A.E. Hotchner's *Papa Hemingway: The Ecstasy and Sorrow* (New York: William Morrow, 1983, 320). Then write a paper on what became of Hemingway in the years that followed Paris. Many believe that the American Dream became a nightmare for Hemingway; that he grew rich, soft, paunchy and undisciplined in his daily living; that **success**—the butlers, chauffeurs, chefs, etc.—**spoiled Ernest Hemingway**, corrupted the artist and ultimately destroyed his talent and uniqueness. Title your paper "Fame Became of Him" (after MacLeish's poem and Raeburn's book).

46

Many believe that the American Dream became a nightmare for Hemingway...

Read along while listening to the Alexander Scourby readings of eight of Hemingway's best short stories including "The Killers," "Fifty Grand," "A Clean, Well-Lighted Place," "The Gambler, the Nun, and the Radio," "The Snows of Kilimanjaro," "The Short Happy Life of Francis Macomber," "The Capital of the World," and "The Undefeated." This selection captures the full range of Hemingway's locales, tone, moods and spirit. Then write an essay comparing Hemingway's short stories with his novels. Which genre do you prefer and why? Comment on the sensitivity, zest and flavor of the Hemingway style. Order the six Scourby cassettes (catalog #CXL504 CX) from Listening Library, One Park Avenue, Old Greenwich, CT 06870-9990. Telephone (800) 243-4504. The cost is $39.95.

47

View the color filmstrip (described below) which analyzes Hemingway's *The Old Man and the Sea*. Then discuss its main points in class prior to reading the story. The filmstrip (catalog #N 85 CFX) can be ordered from Listening Library, One Park Avenue, Old Greenwich, CT 06870-9990. Telephone (800) 243-4504. The cost is $35.00.

48

View the Warner Brothers production of *The Old Man and the Sea* starring Spencer Tracy and featuring cameo appearances by Ernest and Mary Hemingway; then write a paper examining how well (or how poorly) the original story is preserved in the dramatized version. The 87-minute videocassette is available at video rental stores.

49

View the videocassette titled *The Spanish Civil War* as background reading for the novel *For Whom the Bell Tolls*. This color and black-white, five-hour film gives the essential history of the conflict that some historians call a "dress rehearsal for World War II." The film can be ordered from Book-of-the-Month Video, Camp Hill, Pennsylvania 17012-0001. Ask for catalog #2VHS 14-6422. The price is $59.95.

50

In *Death in the Afternoon*, one of the most authoritative treatments of bullfighting in the English language, Hemingway makes this statement:

> There are some things which cannot be learned quickly, and time, which is all we have, must be paid heavily for their acquiring. They are the very simplest things, and because it takes a man's life to know them the little new that each man gets from life is very costly and the only heritage he has to leave.

Write a reaction to this statement from your perspective as a young person.

51

Max Eastman's "Bull in the Afternoon" (*New Republic*, June 7, 1933, 94-97) led to a brawl between Eastman and Hemingway and is therefore the most famous parody of Hemingway style. But there are many other famous parodies of Hemingway including E.B. White's "Across the Street and Into the Grill" (*New Yorker*, October 14, 1950, 28); H.W. Hanemann's "A Farewell to Josephine's Arms—The Hemingway of all Flesh" (in Lowrey Burling's *Twentieth Century Parody: American and British* (New York: Harcourt, Brace, 1960); Wolcott Gibbs' "Death in the Rumble Seat" (*New Yorker*, October 8, 1932, 15), and T.S. Matthews' "Petty Grand" (*New Republic,* February 8, 1928). Read these parodies along with James McKelly's "For Whom the Bull Flows: Hemingway in Parody" (*American Literature,* December, 1989); then write a parody on any of Hemingway's posthumously published books (*A Moveable Feast, Islands in the Stream, The Garden of Eden*), none of which have been parodied. For a starter, see Woody Allen's Hemingway parody—"We had great fun in Spain that year and we traveled and wrote and Hemingway took me tuna fishing and we caught four cans…" in *Getting Even* (1966, Random House).

52

Are the words disheartening and pessimistic, or are they ultimately life-affirming in their reminder that "the sun also rises" and the "earth abides forever" in something of a spiritual triumph?

Man's fleeting life and puny significance are recurring themes in Ecclesiastes 1:1-11, the biblical passage used by Hemingway to title *The Sun Also Rises*. According to these verses of Hebrew poetry, which are thought to be some of the purest in all of literature, all of man's endeavors, thoughts, and emotions are ultimately pointless, futile and meaningless; all is "vanity" means that all is in vain, (**not** that people take inflated pride in themselves or their appearance). Read the *New International* and *King James* versions of Ecclesiastes and write a paper affirming or challenging the Hemingway belief that Ecclesiastes puts man in his proper place. Are the words disheartening and pessimistic, or are they ultimately life-affirming in their reminder that "the sun also rises" and the "earth abides forever" in something of a spiritual triumph? In what ways are the words a paean to the beauty, order and peace of nature? How true are the poet's words, "Meaningless! Meaningless! says the Teacher. Utterly meaningless! Everything is meaningless?"

53

Hemingway believed that marlin fishing was the most exciting and colorful of all the categories of sport fishing, and he fished for the 400-pound blue and white varieties in the Gulf Stream off Cuba for more than 30 years aboard the *Pilar,* his custom built fishing yacht. This provides the setting for Hemingway's *The Old Man and the Sea.* Obtain a print or photograph of Winslow Homer's painting "The Gulf Stream," (which now hangs in the Metropolitan Museum of Art in New York), and describe the painting in a paper. Show the picture (an ancient fishing boat caught in the storm in shark-infested waters) to your class as an introduction to *The Old Man and the Sea.* What thoughts seem to be going on in the fisherman's mind? Does he look the way you imagine Santiago to look?

54

The imprint of the Three Mountains Press in Paris which printed Hemingway's *In Our Time* in 1924 was *Levavi oculos meos in montes* (I have lifted my eyes toward the mountains). It has been suggested that the words might later have served as an epigraph for *A Farewell to Arms.* Write a paper explaining how. First read Carlos Baker's "The Mountain and the Plain" in Baker's *Hemingway: The Writer As Artist,* rev. ed. (Princeton: Princeton University Press, 1963), 94-96, 101-8.

I have lifted my eyes toward the mountains.

55

What became of "Stein's" splendid sense of humor in his later writings?

As a high school student, the young Ernest Hemingway contributed 47 pieces to the school newspaper *The Trapeze*, and literary magazine, *The Tabula*. Read these pieces, collected in Matthew Bruccoli's *Ernest Hemingway's Apprenticeship: Oak Park 1916-1917* (Washington, D.C.: NCR Microcard Editions, 1971), and write an essay on the young Hemingway's writing style. What is imitative of Jack London, Ring Lardner, Carl Sandburg and James Whitcomb Riley? Do his stories show promise and anticipate later material? What became of "Stein's" splendid sense of humor in his later writings? Note: A microfilm entitled *Ernest Hemingway in High School: Writings About and By Ernest Hemingway as They Appeared in the Publications of Oak Park and River Forest High School, 1916-1919* is available on loan from Ms. C. Maziarka, Librarian, Oak Park and River Forest High School, 201 North Scoville Avenue, Oak Park, Illinois 60302. See and comment on another example of Hemingway wit below (from *The Trapeze*):

AIR LINE

The following poem was submitted by Ernest Hemingway:

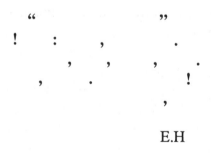

E.H

_____

As you will probably notice the above poem is blank verse.

56

If you can imitate Hemingway's distinctive writing style, you can win dinner for two at one of Hemingway's favorite haunts, Harry's Bar and American Grill at Venice (air transportation provided, of course). The annual International Imitation Hemingway Competition is sponsored by the owners of Harry's Bar and American Grill in San Francisco. A panel of eight judges selects "the best of the worst" of Hemingway parodies in this annual light-hearted contest, the key rule of which is to "sound like Hemingway and read like Hemingway"—to know, as the 1988 winner put it, "that funny is good and very funny is very good." The task for writers is to produce "one really good page of really 'bad' Hemingway." Like Hemingway, you should give care to the shape and ring of your sentences, your words should come quickly, clean and true, and Harry's Bar should be mentioned nicely. Contact Harry's for contest rules and entry deadlines (usually February 1): 500 Van Nesse, San Francisco, California 94102 (415)-86-HARRY.

57

Which of these two artistic triumphs, Guernica *or* For Whom the Bell Tolls, *best rises above the conflict which inspired it and will longest remain a valid protest against all war?*

Two notable artistic achievements growing out of the Spanish Civil War were Hemingway's *For Whom the Bell Tolls* and Pablo Picasso's 12-foot by 26-foot mural titled *Guernica*, which now, after many years in "political exile," hangs at the Prado in Madrid. Although the media are different (print and canvas), the works can still be compared in the statements they make about human folly, nature and insufficiency. Obtain a picture of *Guernica* and explain the work to your class. What event of the war, which claimed more than a million lives, touched Picasso so deeply and inspired such a terrifying and prophetic composition? Which figure represents brutality and darkness (the fascists), and which represents the sufferings of the Spanish people? How does the painting combine personal suffering and universal horror, outrage and protest? What accounts for Hemingway's failure to make fictional use in *For Whom the Bell Tolls* of the saturation bombing and total destruction of Guernica, an undefended Basque market village of no military significance? Which of these two artistic triumphs, *Guernica* or *For Whom the Bell Tolls,* best rises above the conflict which inspired it and will longest remain a valid protest against all war? For an interpretation of *Guernica*, see Mary Mathews Gedo, *Picasso: Art as Autobiography* (Chicago: University of Chicago Press, 1980, 173-189). See also, Roland Penrose, *Picasso: His Life* and Work (Berkeley: University of California Press, 1981, 295-324); Herschel Chipp, *Picasso's Guernica* (n.p., University of California Press, 1988) and Ellen C. Oppler (ed.), *Picasso's Guernica* (n.p., Norton, 1987).

58

"There is hardly a more moving description of kissing in all of fiction," one critic wrote of the scene in *For Whom the Bell Tolls* in which Jordon teaches Maria how to kiss. (See Wayne E. Kvam's *Hemingway in Germany: The Fiction, the Legend, and the Critics* (Athens: Ohio University Press, 1973, 103). Do you agree? Write a paper on Hemingway's description of this expression of affection (which did not become widespread until the A.D. 500s). Include some thoughts on the subject from other famous writers such as Shakespeare, Burns, Tennyson, Yeats, Byron, Oscar Wilde and Jonathan Swift (who exclaimed, "Lord! I wonder what fool it was that first invented kissing).

59

In his 1929 review of *A Farewell to Arms*, J.B. Priestley wrote, "I believe it will not be long before readers will be able to boast of the fact that they bought a first edition of *A Farewell to Arms*." (*Now and Then* 34 Winter 1929, 11-12). Has time proved the reviewer right? Make inquiries with the rare book dealers listed below as to what Hemingway first editions are available and at what prices; then report to the class on your findings. As of this writing, one reputable bookseller offers copy #99 (of 510 deluxe numbered copies signed by Hemingway) of a First Edition at $2,850. The book is in the seldom-seen original glassine, which is chipped and torn, and the original numbered slipcase, which has minor wear. Its condition is "about fine." Another bookseller offers a first edition of *A Farewell to Arms*—a fine copy with tips and edges unrubbed and with some very slight sun tanning" for $1,500. Contact the booksellers below and attempt to find a book in better condition. What prices are asked? While writing, ask for price quotations on first editions of *The Sun Also Rises, For Whom the Bell Tolls,* and *The Old Man and the Sea.* Contact Glenn Horowitz Bookseller, 141 E 44th Street, New York, NY; Pepper & Stein, Rare Books Inc., P.O. Box 2711, Santa Barbara, CA 93120; and George Lenz, Oscar's Bookshop, 389 New York Avenue, Huntington, NY 11743.

"There is hardly a more moving description of kissing in all of fiction..."

...comment on the collection of letters from Hemingway to Adriana Ivancich, the 19-year-old Italian noblewoman who carried on a Platonic affair with Hemingway and who was a model for the heroine Renata in Across the River and Into the Trees.

Read Max Westbook's "Necessary Performance: The Hemingway Collection at Texas" in *The Library Chronicle* (Spring, 1964). Then visit the Harry Ransom Humanities Research Center at the University of Texas at Austin (512) 471-9119 and write a paper on the Hemingway manuscript holdings which include the original holograph manuscript and corrected typescript of *Death in the Afternoon*; 144 letters by Hemingway; an extensive collection of letters exchanged among members of Hemingway's family; and approximately 1,000 volumes of printed books. What are your reactions to the iconography collection of bronze busts by Robert Berks and Larry D. Crowder; the caricature of Hemingway reading Joyce's *Ulysses* at the Stork Club by Albert Herschfeld; and the pencil portrait by George Schreiber? Read and comment on the collection of letters from Hemingway to Adriana Ivancich, the 19-year-old Italian noblewoman who carried on a Platonic affair with Hemingway and who was a model for the heroine Renata in *Across the River and Into the Trees*. In these letters are logged many of the significant events of Hemingway's life between 1950-1955, including his thoughts on the Korean War, the writing and publication of *The Old Man and the Sea,* and his winning of the Nobel Prize.

61

Visit the Manuscripts Department of the Alderman Library at the University of Virginia (Charlottesville), telephone (804) 924-3025. Read the original version (bound page proofs) of A.E. Hotchner's *Papa Hemingway* (for which Mary Hemingway brought a lawsuit); then write a paper detailing how this original version differs from the version that was finally published.

62

Visit the Lilly Library at Indiana University in Bloomington, telephone (812) 335-2452 and write a paper on the Hemingway holdings. Read Hemingway correspondence from May through December, 1918, the approximate timing of his departure from home to participate in World War I until his return after being wounded. The first letter—on the way to the war—is datelined "Somewhere on the Briny." Comment on Hemingway's entire journey including his Paris stopover. Also comment on the self-cartoon of the wounded Hemingway in the July 21 letter.

63

Travel to the Chicago-Detroit-Milwaukee-Grand Rapids area during summer or spring vacation and visit the haunts of the first seventeen summers of Hemingway's youth at Windemere Cottage in northern Michigan, in and about Horton Bay, Petoskey and Walloon Lake. These environs provided the setting and much of the material for "Indian Camp," "The End of Something," "Up in Michigan," "The Three Day Blow," and "Big Two-Hearted River." The summer cottage on Walloon Lake, named (and misspelled) by Hemingway's mother for that picturesque part the English Lake District that inspired Wordsworth and Coleridge, is now designated a historical site by the National Park Service. Write a paper on what you see there.

64

Although proudly an American citizen, Hemingway considered himself first and foremost a "citizen of the world," equally at home in Africa, the Americas, Europe, etc. For a bulletin board display, construct an "Ernest Hemingway Map of the World" indicating the international locales of his real-life travels and fictional adventures. More than 200 locations can be plotted on a world map. Plot any 100 including the following fifteen: Havana, Kilimanjaro, Walloon Lake, Paris, Key West, Oak Park, Sun Valley, Milan, Caporetto, Lausanne, Pamplona, Madrid, El Escorial, Segovia, and Cojimar.

65

Although American citizens are prohibited from visiting Hemingway's *Finca Vigia* outside Havana, now a national museum attracting more than 40,000 visitors per year, there are many published descriptions of the large, white, hacienda-style villa. Consult the sources below and write a description of the house and the surrounding 13 acres. Read James E. Brasch and Joseph T. Sigman, "The Library at *Finca Vigia:* A Preliminary Report, 1977 in *Fitzgerald/Hemingway Annual,* 1978, 184-203. See also Kenneth Tynan, "A Visit to Havana," *Holiday,* 27 (February, 1960), 50-58; Sally Belfrage "Haunted House of Ernest Hemingway," *Esquire,* 59 (February, 1963), 66-67; and Robert Manning, "Hemingway in Cuba,"*The Atlantic Monthly*, 216 (August, 1965), 101-108.

Although proudly an American citizen, Hemingway considered himself first and foremost a "citizen of the world," equally at home in Africa, the Americas, Europe...

66

What became of "'The Sun' Set," the real-life people Hemingway immortalized in *The Sun Also Rises*? Read Bertram D. Sarason's *Hemingway and "The Sun" Set* (Washington, D.C.: NCR Microcard Editions, 1972); then write a paper titled, "The Sun Also Sets: The Real-Life Fates of Harold Loeb (Robert Cohn), Lady Duff Twysden (Lady Brett Ashley), Pat Guthrie (Mike Campbell), Donald Ogden Steward (Bill Gorton) and Montoya. Lady Duff married an American and moved to Santa Fe, where she died at the age of 46. What happened to the others, especially to Cayetano Ordonez (Pedro Romero), Spain's greatest matador of the 1925 season, who suffered the cruelest fate? Read also Harold Loeb's (Robert Cohn's) *The Way It Was* (New York: Criterion, 1959) and James Charters' *This Must Be the Place: Memoirs of Montparnasse* (London: H. Joseph, 1934). Charters was "Jimmy the Barman" at the Dingo Bar.

67

Write a paper giving your impressions of the videotaped interview with Madelaine Hemingway Miller at the Hemingway cottage, Windemere, on Walloon Lake. Some of the interview is taken inside the cottage and includes pictures of Hemingway's guns and an old canoe. Also included are paintings and a musical composition by Hemingway's mother, and remembrances of growing up in rural Michigan (which provided the setting for some of Hemingway's works including "The Battler," "The Last Good Country," "The End of Something," and "The Light of the World"). The 45-minute VHS tape is available ($59.95 plus $3 for postage) from Dave Fortin Productions, P.O. Box 3316, Traverse City, MI 49685.

What became of "The Sun' Set," the real-life people Hemingway immortalized in The Sun Also Rises?

68

Write a critique of the six-hour docudrama titled "Hemingway," shown on American television in May and June, 1988. The film features Stacy Keach in the title role and begins with Hemingway's marriage to Hadley Richardson (Josephine Chaplin) in 1921 and their move to Paris. Gertrude Stein, Ezra Pound, Sherwood Anderson and John Dos Passos are featured. The syndicated miniseries was written and directed by Bernhard Sinkel; producers were Linda Marmelistein, Ully Pickardt and Gerhard von Halem. The cassette is not available for rent or purchase, but home-taped copies are relatively easy to locate.

Hemingway's parents were well-meaning conventional people who were embarrassed by some of the "sordid subjects" he chose to write about.

69

At the time of his wounding in Italy, the eighteen-year-old Hemingway wrote his mother patriotically: "We all offer our bodies and only a few are chosen, but it shouldn't reflect any special credit on those that are chosen. They are just the lucky ones. The mother of a man that has died for his country should be the proudest woman in the world, and the happiest." These grand sentiments provide a forceful contrast to the bitter disillusionment concerning war expressed in *A Farewell to Arms*, written several years later. Read Edwin Campion Vaughan's *Some Desperate Glory: The World War I Diary of a British Officer* (New York: Henry Holt, 1988) for a description of what it was like to come of age in the hard school of the Great War. Then write a paper commenting on Hemingway's remarks to his mother. What do his remarks say about war, growing up, and boyhood soldiering?

70

Hemingway's parents were well-meaning conventional people who were embarrassed by some of the "sordid subjects" he chose to write about. To them, Hemingway's books were not simple and dignified models of English prose that sometimes rose to poetic power, but rather something smutty and embarrassing. They advised their son to look for "joyous, uplifting, optimistic and spiritual" subjects. Even after Hemingway had become famous, his father would sadly exclaim that Ernest had "written another dirty book." Likewise, Hemingway's mother denounced *The Sun Also Rises* as "one of the filthiest books of the year." "Every page," she told him, "fills me with a sick loathing." Write a paper discussing the young artist's obligation (or nonobligation) to give due regard to the sensibilities of parents, family, and friends.

71

Hemingway's preoccupation with death (but lack of morbidity on the subject) can be seen in the following quotation from *Death in the Afternoon:*

> All stories, if continued far enough, end in death; and he is no storyteller who would keep that from you... If two people love each other there can be no happy end to it.

Write a paper reacting to this thought.

72

A skeptic, speaking of Frederic and Catherine in *A Farewell to Arms,* said that they never got "to test their love throughout a long mortgage in suburbia." Would their love have stood the test? Write a short story sequel to *A Farewell to Arms* in which Catherine lives, they return to architecture school (she puts him through), Frederic's drinking becomes a problem, etc. Weave into the story some observations about romantic love (the Frederic and Catherine type), and end the story happily.

73

Write a paper comparing your generation to (a) Hemingway's "Lost Generation," (b) the "beat" generation of the 1950s and (c) the "tune-in, turn-on, drop-out" generation of the late 1960s and 1970s. What sobriquet best describes your own generation? Read Susan Littwin's *The Postponed Generation* (New York: William Morrow, 1986).

74

Opinions differ as to whether Hemingway's suicide in 1961 was an abandonment or a final reaffirmation of the famous Hemingway "Code" which required the hero, although bound to lose, to play the game stoically through to the end. Is the Hemingway dictum that man can be destroyed but not defeated a restatement of Ecclesiastes (the sun also ariseth, the sun goeth down)? Ecclesiastes outlines the tragic nature of life; argues that the meaning of life is beyond the ken of man who dies too soon to learn it; acknowledges the limits of human understanding and the randomness and unfairness of life; and declares that since death overtakes **ALL**, the wise person (who cannot control the forces by which life is shaped), simply makes the best of things. Rather than defiantly accumulating wounds in life, one should enjoy things as they come. Somerset Maugham put it like this in *The Narrow Corner:*

> Life is short, nature is hostile, and man is ridiculous; but oddly enough most misfortunes have their compensations, and with a certain humour and a good deal of horse-sense one can make a fairly good job of what is after all a matter of very small consequence.

Read Charles M. Laymon (ed.), *The Interpreter's One-Volume Commentary on the Bible* (Nashville: Abingdon Press, 1971, 322-323) and R. Gordis, *Koheleth: The Man and His World* (n.p., 1951). Then write a paper taking a position as to whether by the manner of his death Hemingway abandoned or finally reaffirmed the famous Hemingway "Code."

Opinions differ as to whether Hemingway's suicide in 1961 was an abandonment or a final reaffirmation of the famous Hemingway "Code" which required the hero, although bound to lose, to play the game stoically through to the end.

75

Read A.E. Hotchner's *Papa Hemingway: The Ecstasy and Sorrow* (New York: William Morrow, 1983); then write a paper agreeing or disagreeing with Norman Mailer's assessment of Hemingway in "Punching Papa" (*New York Review of Books*, August, 1963, 13).

> It is not likely that Hemingway was a brave man who sought danger for the sake of the sensations it provided him. What is more likely the truth...is that he struggled with his cowardice and against a secret lust to suicide all his life, that his inner landscape was a nightmare, and he spent his nights wrestling with the gods. It may be that...what he failed to do was tragic, but what he accomplished was heroic, for it is possible that he carried a weight of anxiety with him which would have suffocated any man smaller than himself.

It is not likely that Hemingway was a brave man who sought danger for the sake of the sensations it provided him.

76

Hemingway considered various endings to *A Farewell to Arms* before deciding on *The* ending. These endings fall into nine clusters called (1) the *Nada* Ending, (2) the Fitzgerald Ending, (3) the Religious Ending, (4) The Live-Baby Ending, (5) The Morning-After Ending, (6) the Original *Scribner's Magazine* Ending, and (8) *The* Ending. See these variants in Bernard Oldsey's *Hemingway's Hidden Craft: The Writing of 'A Farewell to Arms'*; then write an ending to the book conforming to one of the above variants. A case had been made that Catherine had to die in *The* Ending because of her immorality (a concession to the moralists and book-burners of the day), and that today's more enlightened readers might prefer one of the other endings Hemingway considered but did not use. Facts of publication for the Oldsey book are University Park: Pennsylvania State University Press, 1979. See Chapter 4 and Appendix B.

77

What do you think of the Hemingway quotation below?

> It is not un-natural that the best writers are liars.
> A major part of their trade is to lie or invent and
> they will lie when they are drunk, or to themselves,
> or to strangers. They often lie unconsciously and
> then remember their lies with deep remorse. If
> they knew all other writers were liars too it would
> cheer them up.

How does this jibe with the Hemingway dictum that a writer's job is to tell the truth? Jose Luis Castillo-Puche has made a point that much in Hemingway's life was a lie; that he almost never showed his real self; that most people only scratched the surface of his personality; that he was a pathetically lonely and pathologically devious man; and that beneath the surface, there was boredom, despair, inner emptiness and emotional chaos that made his life a "phenomenal fiasco." Can artists like Hemingway be capable of self-deception, yet incapable of lying about the fundamental human emotions and passions with which their art is concerned? If so, was such the case with Hemingway? Read Castillo-Puche's *Hemingway in Spain* (Garden City, New York: Doubleday, 1974); then write a paper examining Hemingway's essential truthfulness to himself and to his reading public. (The Hemingway quote is from Item #845 in the Hemingway Collection at the John F. Kennedy Library in Boston; Castillo-Puche's assessment is on page xi of his book.)

78

One of Hemingway's greatest fears toward the end of his life was that he had done nothing of lasting worth. What is your opinion? Will Hemingway become dated in an increasingly sophisticated world, or will he remain print-fresh and alive in the imagination for generations to come? Did the *New York Times* writer overstate the case when he called Hemingway the greatest writer since the death of Shakespeare? Write a paper taking either side.

One of Hemingway's greatest fears toward the end of his life was that he had done nothing of lasting worth.

79

The central motifs in Hemingway fiction are death, pride, bravery, fear, struggle, and oblivion. Write a paper exploring the dominant themes in your own thinking.

80

In recent years many students have declared open season on *A Farewell to Arms'* Catherine Barkley claiming that she presents a deplorable stereotype in being a mindless creature who denies her own individuality by dissolving her identity into Frederic's. What do you think of the following statements by Catherine, and what offsetting statements in *A Farewell to Arms* tend to disprove the claim that Catherine is not a "thoroughly modern Millie"? Is it likely that Catherine and Lady Brett (*The Sun Also Rises*) would have been good friends?

    (a)   I'll do what you want and say what you want.

    (b)   There isn't any me anymore. Just what you want.

    (c)   Is there anything I do you don't like? Can I do anything to please you?

    (d)   There isn't any me. I'm you. Don't make up a separate me.

The central motifs in Hemingway fiction are death, pride, bravery, fear, struggle, and oblivion.

81

Carl Jung wrote the following in *Modern Man in Search of a Soul* (London: K. Paul, Trench Trubner, 1933):

> About a third of my cases are suffering from no clinically definable neurosis, but from the sense-lessness and emptiness of their lives. This can be described as the general neurosis of our time.

Jung was writing about the 1920s and 1930s, when Hemingway was coming into his own as a writer. Apply Jung's diagnosis to the "*Sun* set" in *The Sun Also Rises*. What do you think about the vapid conversations, the materialistic outlook, the hedonism, and the aimlessness and lack of direction for Robert Cohn, Lady Brett Ashley, Mike Campbell, and Bill Gorton? Does Jung's diagnosis apply broadly to Hemingway's "Lost Generation" as well? Would the diagnosis fit your own generation today?

82

It has been said that more "critical nonsense" has been written on Hemingway than on any other literary figure.

It has been said that more "critical nonsense" has been written on Hemingway than on any other literary figure. Hemingway himself complained that his work was often overinterpreted by university-based academics and that much of the criticism was trivial and preposterous. For example, critics have asked whether General Custer was a model for the fascist captain in *For Whom the Bell Tolls;* whether there was underlying significance to references to Joe DiMaggio in *The Old Man and the Sea;* whether there was Freudian significance to "Up in Michigan" and "Three Day Blow"; or hidden symbolism in the fact that members of *"The Sun* set" ordered eggs for breakfast in *The Sun Also Rises*? One critic even claimed that the "alcoholic content" of *A Farewell to Arms* was important to "a proper interpretation of its meaning in many of its finer points." Consult Audre Hanneman's *Ernest Hemingway: A Comprehensive Bibliography* (Princeton University Press, 1967) and Linda Welshimer Wagner's *Ernest Hemingway: A Reference Guide* (Boston: G.K. Hall, 1977) for comprehensive listings of what has been written about Hemingway's work. Read several of the more interesting sounding pieces and write a paper on the volume, fairness and depth of Hemingway criticism. Consult also

Jeffrey Meyers' *Hemingway: The Critical Heritage* (London: Routledge & Kegan Paul, 1982) for the acknowledged "best" of Hemingway criticism, and read Fraser Drew's "April 8, 1955, with Hemingway: Unedited Notes on a Visit to *Finca Vigia*," *Fitzgerald/Hemingway Annual, 1970,* 112.

83

Marion Smith, wife of Hemingway's boyhood friend, Bill, (who is Bill Gorton in *The Sun Also Rises*) said:

> Hemingway was a genius about hate as much as he was about writing. He was the greatest hater I ever met and don't forget I'm from Washington.

Smith alluded to the fact that except for Ezra Pound, Hemingway turned on virtually everyone who had ever helped or befriended him in any way, including his own mother, Sherwood Anderson, Gertrude Stein, Ford Madox Ford, Max Eastman, Scott Fitzgerald, Archibald MacLeish, Gerald Murphy and John Dos Passos. Does this lend support to Raymond Schroth's statement that in Hemingway's life, "one of the allegedly most romantic lives in our time, there was so little generosity...so little lasting love"? Do you agree with Harold Loeb (Robert Cohn in *The Sun Also Rises)* that even at age twenty-six, Hemingway was "already too sick for friendship." Read Bertram Sarason's *Hemingway and "The Sun" Set* (Washington, D.C., NCR Microcard Editions, 1972), and listen to the National Public Radio Cassette "Mary Hemingway: Life with Ernest" (Order by telephone 608-263-4892, $10.95); then write a paper reacting to the above quotations.

He was the greatest hater I ever met and don't forget I'm from Washington.

84

Hemingway believed in the mending and restoration of the soul through camping trips amid mountains and forests and along running streams. What do you think of the idea of nature as therapy? In "Big Two-Hearted River," Nick comes to Seney in Northern Michigan to recover from shattering war memories. In seeking solace in the healing power of nature, he leaves everything else behind—"the need for thinking, the need to write, other needs," and loses himself in hiking, tenting, fishing and cooking. Write a paper on the rejuvenating powers of nature; the renewal and fresh vigor that can come from escaping civilization, breathing pure air, sleeping well, etc. Draw from your own personal experiences if possible.

Hemingway believed in the mending and restoration of the soul through camping trips amid mountains and forests and along running streams.

85

Make an effort to transform Hemingway's verbal art to another medium, visual art. With oil and canvas, recreate the scenes below:

(A)   *The Sun Also Rises.* Jake, having left Paris to spend a week in Pamplona, describes a train ride through the south of France:

It was a lovely day, not too hot, and the country was beautiful from the start...The grain was just beginning to ripen and the fields were full of poppies. The pastureland was green, and there were fine trees, and sometimes big rivers and chateaux off in the trees.

(B)   *The Old Man and the Sea.* Santiago, the old fisherman, is pulled far out into the Gulf Stream where he finds a universe of consummate splendor and natural beauty—the celestial lights, the flying fish, the blue waves, the warm breezes of southerly latitudes, and Santiago only a tiny speck in the measureless vastness of the universe.

86

Norman Mailer criticized *The Old Man and the Sea* in saying that

> a work of affirmation must contain its moment
> of despair—specifically, there must be a bad
> moment when the old man Santiago is tempted
> to cut the line and let the big fish go. Hemingway
> avoided the problem by never letting the old
> man be seriously tempted.

Read Richard B. Hovey's *Hemingway: The Inward Terrain* (Seattle: University of Washington Press, 1960); then write a paper agreeing or disagreeing with Mailer's criticism. See especially pages 231-232.

87

Write a paper reacting to the *Green Hills of Africa* quotation below (108-109):

> A country, finally, erodes and the dust blows away,
> the people all die and none of them were of any
> importance permanently except those who practiced
> the arts.

...and none of them were of any importance permanently except those who practiced the arts.

88

Paris' Montparnasse was a fountain of postwar freedom for the Lost Generation and an international gathering place for the brainy excitement-seekers whose ranks included writers, painters, degenerates, society women, sailors, nobles, businessmen, etc. For an account of the goings on in the attics, studios, salons, cafes and bars of this international bohemian center, read James Charters' *This Must Be the Place: Memoirs of Jimmie the Barman* (New York: Lee Furman, 1937). Also, order back issues of the *Lost Generation Journal* from Dr. Tom Wood, *LGJ,* Route 5, Box 134, Salem, Missouri 65560 and write a paper on the journal's contributions to an understanding of the period and to Hemingway studies. The following pieces are especially noteworthy:

Paris' Montparnasse was a fountain of postwar freedom for the Lost Generation and an international gathering place for the brainy excitement-seekers ...

Origin of the Term Lost Generation

The Short Unhappy War of Ernest Hemingway

Remembrance of a Paris Long Past

Hemingway's Fascination with Pamplona

Hemingway's Favorite Watering Hole

Hemingway's Wives: You Have to Praise Them

I Should Have Stayed in Paris

Hemingway's Drinking Fixation

Paris Through Wine Colored Glasses

Flashbacks: Paris in the 1920s

Ray Carey: Barman of Montparnasse

Hadley: An Engaging Person

Expatriate Little Magazines Were Beacons

I Have Always Been Drawn Back to Paris

89

Somerset Maugham, who, like Hemingway, exerted substantial influence on the literature of his time, once said that his stories proposed "only to offer entertainment, which I still think, impertinently, is the main object of a work of fiction." Write a paper reacting to this statement and considering whether Hemingway attempted more, and if so, how and in what ways he succeeded (failed).

...Brett became a role model for a generation of American college girls.

90

As one of the greatest female characters in all of literature, Lady Brett (*The Sun Also Rises*), represents one of Hemingway's finest triumphs. A promiscuous heroine of the Flapper Age, she presided over a hard-drinking entourage of youth in Hemingway's novel and became the female symbol for the Lost Generation. As a libertine who bobbed her hair, wore slacks, and drank along with the men, Brett became a role model for a generation of American college girls. Write a character study of Lady Brett after reading Harold Loeb's (Robert Cohn's) *The Way It Was* (Criterion, 1959) and James Charters' *This Must Be The Place: Memoirs of Montparnasse* (London: H. Joseph, 1934). Charters ("Jimmy the Barman" at the Dingo Bar) wrote that Lady Brett (Duff) was "natural, genuinely kind, unpretentious, intuitive, gentle, aristocratic, and of course, doomed." He remembered her affectionately with the following words: "She married a loving husband and I'm sure both lived very happily together until the Almighty chose to take Duff into his loving care. God bless her, and may her soul rest in peace." Read also Bertram D. Sarason's *Hemingway and "The Sun" Set* (NCR Microcard Ed., 1972).

...Lady Brett (Duff) was "natural, genuinely kind, unpretentious, intuitive, gentle, aristocratic, and of course, doomed."

91

Read Activity #70 and answer the questions posed in it after considering the following generalizations about artists:

...part of the artist's pain is that he is not and cannot be like other people.

(1)   Artists work exclusively for themselves. They seek no applause and attach no importance to considerations of style and fashion. They are necessarily selfish.

(2)   The artist deals with fundamental human emotions, passions, aspirations and ideals; knows man's deepest longings and desires; and is utterly incapable of lying on these subjects.

(3)   Artists live at an angle to life and therefore see it more clearly.

(4)   Artistic genius is a double-edged gift, for those who have it are condemned to difficult and solitary lives.

(5)   Artists are possessed of a nature which seeks its own torment.

(6)   Pain and art are inseparable, and part of the artist's pain is that he is not and cannot be like other people.

Include in your paper a discussion of the conditions that must be present for art to flourish. The socialist view of art, for example, is that politics is the most important subject for artists, and that artists should bend their talents to consolidating the revolution and reconstructing society. Art outside these boundaries is self-indulgent and decadent. Can art flourish under such conditions? Could the apolitical Hemingway have written under such conditions?

92

Read Activity #70 and write a paper discussing what constitutes "good" literary taste. Take into account that the reaction of much of middle America to *A Farewell to Arms* was negative as can be seen from the following excerpts from two letters to *Scribner's Magazine* after serialization of *A Farewell to Arms:*

> I am discontinuing my subsubscription to a magazine which I have read since its first number...your choice of fiction is most distasteful. Specifically I object to this serial 'A Farewell to Arms,'...I cannot allow a magazine containing such vileness to be seen in my house. I have burned the offending number. There is no excuse for printing indecency.

> It is with keen regret that I am now obliged (to cancel my subscription)...I refer particularly to Ernest Hemingway's *A Farewell to Arms,* which in my judgment, is absolutely lacking in literary merit and vulgar beyond expression. Everyone who thinks realizes that such conditions exist, but why a magazine like yours should exploit such disgusting situations, is hard to understand.

See these and other criticisms of *A Farewell to Arms* in Michael Reynolds' *Hemingway's First War: The Making of A Farewell to Arms* (Princeton University Press, 1976).

NOTES

NOTES

BACKGROUND INFORMATION AND FURTHER STUDY

STUDENTS' CORNER

Here are some interesting comments my students have made in class or on paper.

Hemingway read Ecclesiastes at a young age and it must have hit him like a truck. He knew it was true and he didn't like it. It stunned him and I don't think he ever got over it. All those "nada, nada" sighs came from Ecclesiastes really. He just repackaged it, and ironically in doing so he proved again the main point in Ecclesiastes. There really isn't anything new under the sun.

I agree with "Old Mellifluous" (Hemingway's nickname for William Faulkner). He really did find God at the end *(The Old Man and the Sea)*. I'm so glad. In a lot of ways, he was like an adolescent for a long time. This (Old Man) just shows that he finally grew up. I don't mean in a religious sense necessarily.

Don't try to give Hemingway a social conscience. You can't find it in *For Whom the Bell Tolls*, or in *To Have and Have Not* for that matter. If he had had one, he wouldn't have built a $20,000 swimming pool during the depression when half the country was out of work and the other half was making $30 a month.

Frederic was right at the end *(A Farewell to Arms)*. I would have felt the same way. There isn't any rhyme or reason for anything, really. Most of us adjust to that sooner or later on an intellectual level. But our emotional side tells us it's better to look on the bright side.

I don't think his being married all that many times proves anything except that he was trying to prove his manhood.

As a woman, I couldn't have lived with Hemingway. I couldn't take the moody spells or the mean streak. You can just go so far. I know you have to make allowances for geniuses—not always hold them to the same standards. They are entitled to their quirks. I just couldn't live like that. That wouldn't be any life for me. He should have given his war medals to his wives. They deserved them more than he did.

I like Hemingway. But I wish he had written something on the other side too—something inspiring, comforting and spiritually nourishing—like how to have a meaningful life. Just surviving is not enough for me.

Hemingway never found any meaning in life but you have to admire him for looking honestly and sincerely. All our souls are hungry for some meaning; we want a life that matters; we want the world to be different because we lived. I don't think he was a pessimist. He was an optimist really. He never quit looking for answers. He played it straight. He tried for the truth. He plugged away to the end. That's optimism.

Reading Hemingway cures you of unrealistic expectations about the world.

Every book Hemingway wrote was a protest against Ecclesiastes, against dying and being forgotten, against being "here today and gone tomorrow." He wrote because he wanted to live on through his books. He was a tiny voice crying out, "I was here, remember me, don't forget." But down deep he knew the preacher was right: All is vanity. Maybe that's why he killed himself.

I think his Puritan upbringing left him with a fear that somehow, someway there just might be somebody around who was happy and enjoying life. He set out to correct the problem.

Hemingway's view of life was tragic and we have to make room in our thinking for that point of view. Otherwise we will never grow up.

The public thinks of Hemingway as a **bon vivant**, citizen of the world and all that. But really, in a lot of ways he was a man without a country, without a religion, and without a family. He was a very lonely man. Scott Fitzgerald was right: "Show me a hero and I'll write you a tragedy."

I don't think he had a right to such a bleak view of life. He grew up in a good home in a good neighborhood; he had all the advantages; he could have gone to college if he had wanted to. Not all of us can. I think a lot of people are entitled to his view of life, but not him.

The Sun Also Rises helped usher in the modern world with flappers and bobbed hair and all that. Hemingway did as much as anybody to kill off the Victorian era. But now the era he helped to create is as jaded to us as the Victorian age was to him. No one believes all his bunkum about women, war, and manhood anymore. Really, one generation **does** passeth away, and another generation cometh.

Will we remember Hemingway more for how he expressed himself than for what he said? Isn't what someone says more important than how he says it? Isn't substance to be preferred over style?

I can see the same chaos in the world Hemingway saw. But a stiff upper lip is not enough for me. Supposedly we have the ability to think and reason to change things, to improve the world. I think he gave up too soon. Hemingway said it himself, "The world's a fine place and worth fighting for." We are not victims of forces too powerful to fight. The human race needs more Davids (who will stand up to Goliath).

I think those hundreds of accidents he had over his lifetime were more booze related than evidence of a death wish. He was drinking before breakfast every morning. His life really fit the definition of tragedy where greatness and weakness are intermingled on a path to ruin.

My first introduction to Hemingway occurred when I was fourteen during a stroll through the shelves of a public library. My fingers fell enthusiastically upon the simple dialogue and easy print of a book entitled *The Sun Also Rises* (the cover also had a nice painting on it). Because I am very much one who **does** judge a book by its cover (and its size of print), I snapped it up. Little did I know that I would finish the book in two nights and be scurrying back for such delicacies as *A Farewell to Arms, Green Hills of Africa, To Have and Have Not, The First Forty-Nine Stories, Islands in the Stream,* and *The Old Man and the Sea.*

For me, Hemingway's books are works to be read on summer afternoons (spring in Texas) when your room is full of sleepy sunlight and you've just awakened from a nap—and of course a pitcher of lemonade is within easy reach.

It is good not to have any seriously set philosophies in your head because, chances are, he will leave you feeling pretty stupid for thinking that you know what's going on.

If something in a book happens that doesn't make it a happy ending, don't get depressed—Ernest is just being Ernest. He'll do that to you if you're the type to pray for happy endings. And perhaps if you look deeply enough they really are happy endings—just not from the common angle. Sometimes it takes a great deal to understand Ernest. He is a very complicated man.

There's a parallel between Hemingway's life and Harry's (*The Snows of Kilimanjaro*) in that Harry had too much money and gave in to the good life, the fast lane, the international sporting set, etc., and then grew dependent on it and died artistically long before his physical death. Didn't the same thing happen to Hemingway?

CHRONOLOGY

1899

Ernest Hemingway is born in Oak Park, Illinois, a Chicago suburb, on July 21.

1913

Enters eighth grade at Oak Park where he participates in a variety of sports including boxing and football. Hemingway is an above-average, but not outstanding student.

1916

Becomes editor of the school newspaper, *The Trapeze*, and writes for the school literary magazine, *The Tabula*.

1917

Graduates from Oak Park; is rejected for military service in the First World War because of poor vision; becomes a reporter for the *Kansas City Star*. Here he developed a spare, journalistic writing style that would become his trademark.

1918

Becomes volunteer ambulance driver with Italian army. Seriously wounded on July 8. Convalesces in a Milan hospital and carries on relationship with Agnes H. von Kurowsky on whom he modeled Catherine Barkley in *A Farewell to Arms*.

1919

Returns to the United States. Joins staff of the *Star Weekly* in Toronto.

1921

Marries Hadley Richardson in September. They move to Paris where Hemingway works as a correspondent for the *Star Weekly*.

1922

Meets Ezra Pound, Archibald MacLeish, and Gertrude Stein in Paris. All influenced his writing.

1923

Visits Spain and begins life-long interest in bullfighting. Begins collecting notes for what will become *Death in the Afternoon*. Hemingway's first book, *Three Stories and Ten Poems,* is published in Paris. (Includes "My Old Man.") Returns to Toronto for birth of first son, John (Bumby).

1924

Three Mountains Press in Paris publishes *In Our Time*. Hemingway returns to Pamplona for fiesta and follows the bullfight circuit.

1925

Meets Cayetano Ordonez (Nino de la Palma) on whom the matador Pedro Romero will be modeled in *The Sun Also Rises. In Our Time* is published in New York. (Includes "Indian Camp," "A Very Short Story," and "Big Two-Hearted River.")

1926

Charles Scribner's Sons of New York becomes Hemingway's publisher for life with *Torrents of Spring* and *The Sun Also Rises*.

1927

Divorced from Hadley Richardson; marries Pauline Pfeiffer; takes up residence in Key West. *Men Without Women* is published. (Includes "Now I Lay Me.") "Fifty Grand" is published in *Atlantic Monthly* in July. "The Killers" is published in *Scribner's Magazine* in March.

1928

Begins writing *A Farewell to Arms*. Patrick (second son) is born in Kansas City. Visits Havana for first time. Father commits suicide.

1929

Scribner's brings out *A Farewell to Arms*.

1931

Gregory (third son) is born in Kansas City.

1932

Hemingway lives, fishes and writes in Key West. *Death in the Afternoon* is published.

1933

Goes to Africa on safari with Pauline Pfeiffer. *Winner Take Nothing* is published. (Includes "The Gambler, The Nun, and The Radio," titled "Give Us a Prescription, Doctor" when it first appeared in *Scribner's Magazine* in April). "A Clean Well-Lighted Place" is published in *Scribner's Magazine* in March.

1934

Works on *The Green Hills of Africa*. Commissions building of his fishing yacht, *Pilar*. The name will be used in *For Whom the Bell Tolls*.

1935

The Green Hills of Africa is published. Hemingway has fishing experiences in the Gulf Stream that will appear later in *The Old Man and the Sea*.

1936

Civil War breaks out in Spain; Hemingway sides with the Republicans. "On the Blue Water" (later expanded into *The Old Man and the Sea*) is published by *Esquire* in April. "The Capital of the World" appears in *Esquire* under title, "The Horns of the Bull" in June. "The Snows of Kilimanjaro" appears in *Esquire* in August. "The Short Happy Life of Francis Macomber" appears in *Cosmopolitan* in September. Hemingway meets Martha Gellhorn, who will become his third wife.

1937

Hemingway goes to Spain as war correspondent. Collaborates with John Dos Passos and Archibald MacLeish in filming "The Spanish Earth." Helps raise money for the Republican cause. *To Have and Have Not* is published.

1939

Settles permanently in Cuba and begins writing *For Whom the Bell Tolls*.

1940

Hemingway is divorced from Pauline Pfeiffer and marries Martha Gellhorn. Buys *Finca Vigia* outside Havana, which will be his home until 1960. *For Whom the Bell Tolls* is published.

1941

Visits China, Indochina and the Philippines. Begins patrolling Cuban waters for German submarines in *Pilar*.

1942

Men at War is published by Crown Publishers in New York.

1944

Meets *Time* writer Mary Welsh, who will become his fourth wife.

1945

Returns to Cuba from duties as war correspondent in Europe for *Collier's*. Is divorced from Martha Gellhorn.

1946

Marries Mary Welsh in Havana.

1950

Across the River and Into the Trees is published to generally unfavorable reviews.

1951

Hemingway's mother and Pauline Pfeiffer die.

1952

The Old Man and the Sea is published to world-wide acclaim, spiking rumors that Hemingway is "washed-up" as a writer.

1953

Receives Pulitzer Prize for Literature. Returns to Spain for first time since the Civil War. Survives two airplane crashes in Africa.

1954

Awarded Nobel Prize for Literature.

1959

Returns to Spain to follow the bullfight circuit. Publicly declares support for the Cuban revolution.

1960

The Dangerous Summer is published in *Life* September 5, 12, and 19. Hemingway becomes increasingly depressed and paranoiac. Enters Mayo Clinic in Rochester, Minnesota, for electroshock treatment.

1961

Dies from self-inflicted gunshot wound on July 2. Mary Hemingway donates *Finca Vigia* to the Cuban government, to be used as the Hemingway Museum.

NOTES

FILMOGRAPHY

*A Farewell To Arms (Paramount 1932) Gary Cooper and Helen Hayes

The Spanish Earth (Contemporary Historians 1937)

For Whom the Bell Tolls (Paramount 1943) Gary Cooper and Ingrid Bergman. Not currently in distribution. Owned by Swank Motion Pictures, 201 S. Jefferson, St. Louis, MO 63166 (314) 534-6300

*To Have and Have Not (Warner Brothers 1944) Humphrey Bogart and Lauren Bacall

**The Killers (Universal 1946) Burt Lancaster and Ava Gardner. Available in 16 mm for rental ($75) from Swank Motion Pictures, 201 S. Jefferson, St. Louis, MO 63166 (314) 534-6300

The Macomber Affair (United Artists 1947) Robert Preston and Gregory Peck)

Under My Skin *My Old Man* (Twenty Century-Fox 1950) John Garfield

The Breaking Point *To Have and Have Not* (Warner Brothers 1950) John Garfield and Patricia Neal

*The Snows of Kilimanjaro (Twentieth Century-Fox 1952) Gregory Peck and Susan Hayward

*The Sun Also Rises (Twentieth Century-Fox 1957) Tyrone Power and Ava Gardner

A Farewell to Arms (Twentieth Century-Fox 1957) Rock Hudson and Jennifer Jones

The Gun Runners *To Have and Have Not* (United Artists 1958) Audie Murphy and Eddie Albert

The Old Man And The Sea (Warner Brothers 1958) Spencer Tracy

Hemingway's Adventures of a Young Man (Twentieth Century-Fox 1962) Arthur Kennedy, Jessica Tandy and Paul Newman

*The Killers (Universal-International 1964) Lee Marvin, Angie Dickinson and Ronald Reagan

Islands in the Stream (Paramount 1977) George C. Scott and Claire Bloom

(* = Videocassette Available For Rent Or Purchase)

(** = Film Available For Rent)

FURTHER READING

Asselineau, Roger (ed.). *The Literary Reputation of Hemingway In Europe* (Paris: Lettres Modernes—M.J. Minard, 1965).

Baker, Carlos (ed.). *Ernest Hemingway: Critiques of Four Major Novels* (New York: Charles Scribner's Sons, 1962).

Baker, Carlos. *Hemingway: The Writer As Artist* (Princeton: Princeton University Press, 1972).

Baker, Carlos (ed.). *Hemingway and His Critics: An International Anthology* (New York: Hill and Wang, 1961).

Brenner, Gerry. *Concealments in Hemingway's Works* (Columbus: Ohio State University Press, 1983).

Brian, Denis. *The True Gen: An Intimate Portrait of Hemingway by Those Who Knew Him* (New York: Grove Press, 1988).

Broer, Lawrence R. *Hemingway's Spanish Tragedy* (University: University of Alabama Press, 1973).

Bruccoli, Matthew J. *Ernest Hemingway's Apprenticeship: Oak Park, 1916-1917* (Washington, D.C.: NCR Microcard Editions, 1971).

Bruccoli, Matthew J. *Conversations with Ernest Hemingway* (Jackson: University Press of Mississippi, 1986).

Castillo-Puche, Jose Luis. *Hemingway in Spain* (Garden City, New York: Doubleday, 1974).

Fenton, Charles A. *The Apprenticeship of Ernest Hemingway: The Early Years* (New York: Viking, 1954).

Ferrell, Keith. *Ernest Hemingway: The Search for Courage* (New York: M. Evans, 1984).

Fuentes, Norberto. *Hemingway in Cuba* (Secaucus, N.J.: Lyle Stuart, 1984).

Gajdusek, Robert E. *Hemingway's Paris* (New York: Charles Scribner's Sons, 1978).

Gellens, Jay. *Twentieth Century Interpretations of A FAREWELL TO ARMS,* (Englewood Cliffs, N.J.: Prentice-Hall, 1970).

Gurko, Leo. *Ernest Hemingway and the Pursuit of Heroism* (New York: Thomas Y. Crowell, 1968).

Hanneman, Audre. *Ernest Hemingway: A Comprehensive Bibliography* (Princeton, N.J.: Princeton University Press, 1967).

Hemingway, Gregory H. *Papa: A Personal Memoir,* (Boston: Houghton Mifflin, 1976).

Hemingway, Mary Welsh. *How It Was* (New York: Alfred A Knopf, 1976).

Hotchner, A.E. *Papa Hemingway: The Ecstasy and Sorrow* (New York: William Morrow, 1983).

Hovey, Richard B. *Hemingway: The Inward Terrain* (Seattle: University of Washington Press, 1968).

Killinger, John *Hemingway and the Dead Gods* (n.p.: University of Kentucky Press, 1960).

Kvam, Wayne E. *Hemingway in Germany: The Fiction, the Legend, and the Critics* (Athens: Ohio University Press, 1973).

Laurence, Frank M. *Hemingway and the Movies* (Jackson: University Press of Mississippi, 1981).

Meyers, Jeffrey. *Hemingway: A Biography* (New York: Harper and Row, 1985).

Meyers, Jeffrey (ed.). *Hemingway: The Critical Heritage* (London: Routledge & Kegan Paul, 1982).

Nahal, Chaman. *The Narrative Pattern in Ernest Hemingway's Fiction* (Ruthford: Fairleigh Dickinson University Press, 1971).

Noble, Donald R. *Hemingway: A Revaluation* (Troy, New York: Whitson, 1983).

Oldsey, Bernard. *Hemingway's Hidden Craft: The Writing of 'A Farewell to Arms'* (University Park: Pennsylvania State University Press. 1979).

Oldsey, Bernard (ed.). *Ernest Hemingway: The Papers of a Writer* (New York: Garland Publishing, 1981).

Phillips, Gene D. *Hemingway and Film* (New York: Frederick Ungar, 1980).

Reynolds, Michael S. *Hemingway's First War: The Making of A Farewell to Arms* (Princeton: Princeton University Press, 1976).

Sarason, Bertran D. *Hemingway and "The Sun" Set* (Washington, D.C.: NCR Microcard Editions, 1972).

Shaw, Samuel. *Ernest Hemingway* (New York: Fredrick Ungar, 1973).

Sokoloff, Alice Hunt. *Hadley: The First Mrs. Hemingway* (New York: Dodd, Mead & Co., 1973).

Wagner, Linda Welshimer. *Ernest Hemingway: A Reference Guide* (Boston: G.K. Hall, 1977).

Waldhorn, Arthur. *A Reader's Guide to Ernest Hemingway* (New York: Octagon Books, 1978).

Warren, Robert Penn. "Hemingway," *Selected Essays* (New York: Random House, 1954).

Watts, Emily Stipes. *Ernest Hemingway and the Arts* (Urbana: University of Illinois Press, 1971).

West, Ray B., Jr. and Robert Wooster Stallman. *The Art of Modern Fiction* (New York: Rinehart & Comapny, 1956).

White, William (ed.). *Ernest Hemingway—DATELINE: TORONTO* (New York: Charles Scribner's Sons, 1985).

Williams, Wirt. *The Tragic Art of Ernest Hemingway* (Baton Rouge: Louisiana State University Press, 1981).

Wylder, Delbert E. *Hemingway's Heroes* (Albuquerque: University of New Mexico Press, 1969).

HEMINGWAY'S WORKS

Three Stories & Ten Poems (Paris: Contact Editions, 1923; Bloomfield Hills, Michigan: Bruccoli Clark, 1977).

In Our Time (Paris: Three Mountains Press, 1924; Bloomfield Hills, Michigan: Bruccoli Clark, 1977). *In Our Time* (New York: Boni & Liverright, 1925; London: Cape, 1926; revised edition, New York: Scribner's, 1930).

The Torrents of Spring (New York: Scribner's, 1926; Paris: Crosby Continental Editions, 1932; London: Cape, 1933).

The Sun Also Rises (New York: Scribner's, 1926); published as *Fiesta* (London: Cape, 1927).

Men Without Women (New York: Scribner's, 1927).

A Farewell to Arms (New York: Scribner's, 1929; London: Cape, 1929).

Death in the Afternoon (New York: Scribner's, 1932; London: Cape, 1932).

Winner Take Nothing (New York: Scribner's, 1933; London: Cape, 1934).

Green Hills of Africa (New York: Scribner's, 1935; London: Cape, 1936).

To Have and Have Not (New York: Scribner's, 1937; London: Cape, 1937).

The Spanish Earth (Cleveland: J.B. Savage, 1938).

The Fifth Column and the First Forty-nine Stories (New York: Scribner's, 1938; London: Cape, 1939).

For Whom the Bell Tolls (New York: Scribner's, 1940; London: Cape, 1941).

Across the River and Into the Trees (New York: Scribner's, 1950; London: Cape, 1950).

The Old Man and the Sea (New York: Scribner's, 1952; London: Cape, 1952).

A Moveable Feast (New York: Scribner's, 1964; London: Cape, 1964). Posthumous.

Islands in the Stream (New York: Scribner's, 1970; London: Cape, 1970). Posthumous.

The Garden of Eden (New York: Scribner's, 1986). Posthumous.

FOUNDATION READING FOR HEMINGWAY ENTHUSIASTS:

A Suggested Six-Weeks Reading Program

Hemingway readers will be interested in all or most of the works listed below. For those who wish to read (or re-read) in depth, I suggest the following works and reading timetable. Please note that I have abbreviated titles and facts of publication.

WEEK 1

Read the pioneering critical studies by Carlos Baker and Philip Young, including *Hemingway: The Writer as Artist* and *Ernest Hemingway: A Reconsideration*. Also, Jeffrey Meyers' *Hemingway: A Biography* (1985) and Kenneth Lynn's *Hemingway* (1987).

WEEK 2

Read the principal works of Professor Michael S. Reynolds, Department of English, North Carolina State University. The short titles of his works (1976-1986) are *Hemingway's First War, Hemingway's Reading,* and *The Young Hemingway.*

WEEK 3

Read (re-read) Hemingway's primary works—*Sun Rises, Farewell, Bell Tolls, Old Man,* and *Short Stories* (the *Finca Vigia* edition).

WEEK 4

Read Don Noble's *Revaluation,* Baker's *Critiques of Four Major Novels,* and *Hemingway Critics: An International Anthology.*

WEEK 5

Read Emily Stipes Watt's *Ernest Hemingway and the Arts* and Raymond Nelson's *Hemingway: Expressionist Artist.* The entire Week 5 should be devoted to these books and their "Works Cited" because they examine how Hemingway's prose was enriched and deepened by the art he owned and viewed.

WEEK 6

Readings should examine Hemingway, the man. They include wife Mary's *How It Was,* son Gregory's *Personal Memoir,* friend Hotchner's *Papa,* and friend Castillo-Puche's *Hemingway in Spain.*

NOTES

NOTES

ABOUT THE AUTHOR

Barbara Teeter teaches English at Denton (Texas) High School. She is a graduate of the University of Arkansas and earned an M.A. degree (English) from the University of North Texas. She is a National Endowment for the Humanities fellow, and the recipient of numerous teaching awards (Texas Excellence Award for Outstanding High School Teachers) and citations (Massachusetts Institute of Technology, Texas A & M University, and Southern Methodist University). Barbara lives with her husband and son (an airline pilot) in Krum, Texas.

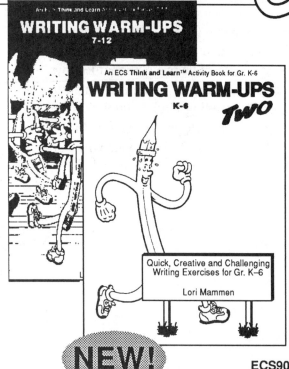

You will love these challenging lessons. The creative activities will motivate even your most reluctant learner.

Tactics to Tackle Thinking:

Creative Activities for the English Classroom

Gr. 7–12

These teaching units show creative methods to include higher-order thinking skills in the secondary English curriculum. Topics include composition, literature, research, skills, vocabulary development and independent projects. More than fifty challenging lessons will motivate your students to think and learn.

ECS9439   Tactics to Tackle Thinking   Grades 7-12 $9.95

NEW!

Springboards for English

33 Creative and Cooperative Lessons
Gr. 6 – 12

These lessons are designed to be springboards for cooperative learning in the language arts classroom. The lessons address a variety of <u>basic skills</u> in a creative, challenging, and cooperative way. Topics include vocabulary development, elaboration strategies, figurative language, creative thinking skills, poetry, and grammar. Each of the lessons emphasizes composition, higher level thinking, and cooperative learning in an easy-to-use format.

NEW!

ECS9498   Springboards for English   Grades 6–12 $11.95